My thanks go to Explore Worldwide Ltd who provided this holiday and gave permission for the book to be published. All names have been changed to protect the privacy of individuals.

Valerie Astill

1

RIO DE JANEIRO

Day 1. Saturday 3rd September.

"I think we're being followed," murmured David as we walked towards the underpass. A chill swept over me and I shivered. The short stretch of roadway and pavement running under the bridge to the Rio Sul Shopping Centre suddenly took on the appearance of a dark tunnel, full of menace. I glanced behind me as casually as I could and saw, a short distance away, a middle-aged, scruffy-looking man in dark clothes with matted long hair and beard, gazing unseeingly into the distance. Not far behind him was a younger man in an old raincoat, also staring into space. Otherwise, the street was completely deserted.

"I think you're right," I said. "We ought to look for a shop or café where there are people about." Apart from some small change, we had nothing on us worth stealing and in any case, now that we were aware of their presence, the two of us together would probably have been a match for these men unless they had knives. However, we were overtired, suffering from jetlag and perhaps a little paranoid. Only fifteen minutes earlier, our group leader had impressed on us that we were likely to be mugged in Rio and in the short time since our arrival, we had seen for ourselves how easily a theft can take place.

This end of the street looked quite poor and run-down. Beside us, hoardings surrounded a building site while opposite were what appeared to be terraced houses. Then David spotted a sign over one of the doors. "Look, there's a small hotel over the road. Let's wait in there for a while until it's clear." We crossed over, trying to look unconcerned, deliberately not hurrying, and entered the foyer of the hotel with a sigh of relief.

The receptionist looked up from her desk. "Good morning, may I help you?" she asked in perfect English. "Do you serve morning coffee, please?" "No, I'm sorry," she replied. "Well, do you have a brochure of the hotel please?" Hunting around behind her desk, the receptionist managed to find one and we stood there in the foyer, pretending to study it. After a few moments, David cautiously ventured out and looked around. "It's O.K.," he called to me. "Thanks," I said to the receptionist and putting the brochure back on her desk, I followed him out. There was nobody in sight so, by mutual consent, we hurried back the way we had come.

We had arrived in Rio de Janeiro that morning at the start of a three week tour in South America visiting Brazil, Peru and Bolivia. A group of us had been collected at the airport and taken to our hotel on the Avenida Princesa Isabel in the Leme district of Rio, halfway between the underpass and Copacabana Beach. There were several hotels at this end of the street, all of which appeared to be small family-run establishments, inexpensive-looking but clean and well cared-for, interspersed with small shops and office blocks.

As we entered the hotel, we saw to the left of the foyer a partially screened off area where wooden chairs were set around small tables with the reception counter situated on the far right. Carol, our group leader, told us to put our cases together in the centre of the foyer and to sit at the tables to fill in the paperwork required for the hotel records while she checked us all in.

Once we had had time to complete the forms, Carol said, "O.K. everyone. When I call out your name and room number, hand your form with your passport to Reception and collect your key. You'll have about half an hour to take your luggage to your rooms and freshen up and then we'll meet in the conference room on the first floor at half past ten. Bring along your insurance details. We can all introduce ourselves and I'll tell you a little about what to expect on the holiday. Right, James Bexon, Room 257."

James walked over to the counter, picked up his key and turned to collect his luggage. A look of shock and disbelief appeared on his face. "Where's my bag?" he cried. "It was here a moment ago! I left it right on top of the cases." His gaze swept around the foyer. "It's a flight bag in tan leather with tartan sides," he said helplessly. "Has anyone moved it?" We stared at him in stunned silence for a few seconds and then three of the party, Graham, Karl and Phil, jumped to their feet.

"Quick," Graham said to Karl, "you look down the corridor while I check outside." He looked outside the entrance to the hotel, where passers-by were hurrying along the street, going uncaringly about their own business. Karl peered down the corridor at the back of the foyer while Phil and James checked round the Reception area. Needless to say, there was no sign of the missing hand luggage.

"What am I going to do?" asked James despairingly. "That bag had all my cash and travellers cheques in it." Then, realising the extent of the problem, "I've lost my passport, flight tickets and camera equipment as well. That equipment was new. It cost me several thousand pounds. I'll never get it back on insurance." Not one of us had seen anything suspicious and it made us realise how careful we would have to be. James naturally wanted immediate action taken to recover his property but Carol told him firmly that he would have to wait while she attended to the needs of the party as a whole.

Later, in the conference room, we all sat round a long table and briefly introduced ourselves to the others in the group. Carol started off the proceedings. She was tall and attractive with long blonde hair, and told us that she spoke fluent Spanish and Portuguese and had been out in South America as a tour leader since leaving university four years earlier. She was engaged to be married and this was to be her last tour. It was then the turn of the rest of the group. Luckily, David and I were among the first to introduce ourselves and I was then able to relax and take an interest in everyone else.

James was a young businessman from London in his mid-twenties, full of charm and with an engaging smile; Phil was a gas fitter in his early twenties from Sussex; Graham, a cheerful middle-aged bachelor from Yorkshire, was travelling with Karl from Bavaria, a tall, slightly gangly young man in his twenties who spoke excellent English and had met and made friends with Graham on a previous holiday with the same tour company; Jack and Jean in their mid-forties came from Hampshire; while Michael and his wife Lynne, in their thirties, were from Lancashire. David and I, in our fifties, were the veterans of the group.

After telling us that six more people would be arriving to join our group later in the day, Carol gave us a brief run-down of the whole itinerary and then more detailed information about Rio.

"Rio de Janeiro means 'January River'," she began. "It was discovered and named in January 1502 by a Portuguese sea captain, André Gonçalves, who anchored in the bay but mistakenly thought he was in a river estuary. By the end of the 16th century, the Portuguese had built a town here and were exporting wood and sugar cane. Gold was discovered in a neighbouring state at the beginning of the 18th century, followed shortly afterwards by a boom in the popularity of coffee and, as a result, Rio rapidly increased in size and prosperity." She told us that Rio had replaced Salvador de Bahia as the capital of Brazil in 1763, remaining the capital until 1960 when that honour had passed to the new city of Brasilia.

"Rio's citizens are known as Cariocas," she continued. "They call their town the Cidade Marvilhosa with good reason because, as you will see, it is situated in a wonderful position between the mountains and the sea and is famous for its sandy beaches and, of course, its Carnival. However it also has its less attractive side. People flock here from the countryside looking for jobs and they have thrown up shanty towns known as favelas on the hillsides around the city. These people are unskilled and find it very difficult to get work. They have to survive in any way they can so you will need to keep alert and watch your belongings at all times. Make sure you leave any jewellery, travellers cheques and other valuables in the hotel safe and only take a small amount of cash with you, to hand over if the necessity arises."

Carol gave us each an outline tourist map of the city showing the areas and names of the main streets and pointed out where our hotel was located on the map. The talk finished at about 11.30am and we were free for the rest of the day. This gave Carol the opportunity to take James to the local police station to report the theft of his hand luggage, help him to sort matters out with his insurance company and obtain replacement travellers cheques and flight tickets. Luckily he had a photocopy of his passport in his suitcase.

Before leaving the hotel, David and I followed Carol's advice and locked away everything that might conceivably be thought valuable, including our cheap plastic watches, venturing out empty handed with only a small amount of cash spread around various pockets. Our sketch map of the city showed the nearby Rio Sul shopping centre where we had decided to start our explorations but after our slight scare near the underpass, we decided instead to head in the opposite direction towards Copacabana Beach and to buy a picnic lunch on the way.

We found a small food store and went inside where we found that all the goods were on shelves behind a counter, well out of reach of customers. We queued at the counter behind a young man who was just putting his purchases into a carrier bag. "Do you speak English?" David asked the assistant, neither of us speaking any Portuguese. "Certainly," came the reply. We asked for some rolls, cheese, tomatoes and bottled water and the girl wrote down the details and the prices, tore the sheet off the pad and handed us the slip of paper.

As we waited, expecting her to collect the items together, a voice behind us said, "Excuse me." Turning round, we saw a pleasant-looking middle-aged Brazilian lady in a smart dark blue woollen suit, wearing expensive-looking jewellery and a gold watch. "My name is Leila," she said. "You have to pay the bill and bring back the receipt to collect your order. If you wait for a moment, I will show you."

She quickly placed her own order and then took us to a cash desk, hidden behind a glass safety screen. We paid our bill, waited until Leila had also paid and then returned with her to queue again at the original counter with the receipts. "This seems a long-winded way of doing things." David was getting bored. "I should imagine that with the high crime rate, it's necessary otherwise the smaller shops would go out of business," I said.

Outside the store, Leila told us that she had lived in Rio for thirty years and worked part-time in an office. We recounted our experiences since we had arrived that morning. "If Rio is this dangerous, aren't you afraid to go outside wearing all that jewellery?" I asked. "It is safe for me because I am a local,", she replied, "but it would not be safe for you because people can see that you are foreigners." She then scribbled something on a piece of paper which she pressed into my hand. "This is my telephone number," she said. "Please ring me if you need any assistance during your stay in Rio." Feeling almost overwhelmed by her friendliness to two complete strangers, we thanked Leila, waved her goodbye and continued on our way to the beach carrying the plastic bag containing our lunch.

It was only a few minutes walk to the Avenida Atlântica which runs along the seafront. The road was very wide with three carriageways in either direction although there was very little traffic about. On the large central reservation, stalls erected under the palm trees displayed wood carvings and large, colourful scarves. These were very attractive but we were surprised by how expensive they were.

The pavements on either side of the avenue were beautifully patterned in Portuguese style, with small black and white cobble stones in a wave design, while at various intervals along the front were time and temperature indicators which showed that it was now early afternoon and a pleasant 72° Fahrenheit. A warm salty breeze blew off the sea and, comfortable in our thin T-shirts and cotton trousers, we were surprised to see the local people wearing heavy winter coats and scarves. Then we realised this was their winter.

A low wall separated the pavement from Copacabana Beach and we sat on this, under the shade of some palm trees growing out of the fine, honey-coloured sand. In front of us, the beach sloped almost imperceptibly for about a hundred yards to the calm blue of the Atlantic Ocean. During the height of the season, from Christmas until Carnival in February or March, the beach would be packed but today the weather was apparently too cold for most people. Apart from a few playing ball games, the sands were nearly deserted.

We noticed that the one or two hardy souls who ventured into the sea left no belongings behind on the beach, not even a towel. We saw later that after swimming, they walked back through the city to their offices, apartments or hotels in wet costumes and with bare feet.

As we ate our picnic, we studied the map and discussed how best to spend the afternoon. David suggested taking a bus to the Botanical Gardens. "They're on the far side of the town," he said "and it'll help us to get our bearings." I thought this was a good idea but finding which bus we needed and where to catch it proved quite a problem. Everyone we asked was very helpful but gave us conflicting information.

Eventually we found a bus-stop in a busy street running parallel to the seafront and a young girl waiting at the stop confirmed it was the right one for the Botanical Gardens. Before long the bus arrived and we found we had to board at the rear of the vehicle. We paid our fare to the conductor and asked him to let us know when we reached our destination before making our way through a turnstile to our seats. "This is different," said David. "At least the conductor knows everyone has paid their fare".

The bus took us along the busy main shopping streets of Copacabana, Ipanema, Leblon and Gavea as we tried to follow our route through the city on the outline map. Most of the other passengers gazed silently out of the windows, immersed in their own thoughts. An elderly gentleman read the newspaper and two women sitting side by side, muffled in thick winter coats and woollen scarves, quietly exchanged the latest gossip. Looking down the side streets to the left, we caught occasional glimpses of the sea. The shops looked interesting and the streets here were vibrant with colour and swarming with people and traffic.

We lost our place on the map at one point so David asked the couple sitting in the seat in front of us if they would mind indicating where we were. They were only too pleased to try to help, chatting to us for the rest of the journey, pointing out places of interest and telling us when we were close to our destination.

It was 4pm by the time we reached the Botanical Gardens. We found the entrance but the ticket kiosk was empty. "Do you think we ought to go in without paying?" asked David. "There's nobody to take our money," I pointed out, "but the gardens still appear to be open so we might as well see what we can now that we're here."

We wandered inside along straight asphalt pathways between trees and shrubs, most of which were labelled with their names and countries of origin. Despite the fact that few plants were in flower at this time of the year, there was a fresh green smell of vegetation in the air and the gardens were a quiet oasis in the midst of the concrete city. Unfortunately, we only had about half an hour before dusk began to fall. "We'd better go," I said. "We need to find where to catch the bus back to Leme." This turned out to be only a few minutes walk along the road. The first two buses to pull up were going to other destinations but our bus came after about twenty minutes, by which time it was nearly dark.

Back at the hotel, we met the rest of our party. Nigel in his twenties worked at the British Embassy in New York; Bob and Mary plus Steve and Betty were two down-to-earth Australian couples of about our own age; and the group was completed by Shelagh, a very slim, dark-haired Canadian policewoman in her early thirties.

That evening, Carol took us all to a local fish restaurant. The menu was in Portuguese and as none of us apart from Carol spoke the language, she was kept busy translating. The waiters were very helpful; they brought across various dishes ordered by other people for us to look at and showed us where they appeared on the menu. We were not quite sure what to expect when we placed our orders as both the names and appearance of some of the dishes were strange to us but when the food finally arrived, it was excellent. I tried red snapper which was delicious and David had a tasty mixed fish bake.

Some of the others tried dishes such as octopus stewed in local wine or bacalhau which turned out to be dried, salted cod, very tasty when cooked with a cheese sauce. We made a note of some basic "menu" Portuguese to help us order future meals and we tried the national drink, caipirinha, made with sugar cane liqueur, lime and ice which was delicious and very refreshing.

During the meal, Jack and Jean told us how they had been walking along the beach that afternoon when a youth had appeared beside them, grabbed Jean's arm, unfastened her watch and run off with it. "We were so shocked that we just stood there and watched him go," said Jack. Luckily, the watch had been inexpensive, but the incident had shaken them.

We finished the meal with coffee and having slept very little on the flight from England, most of us were ready to return to the hotel soon afterwards. David and I were still feeling rather nervous after all the warnings about crime so after checking that the door to our room was locked, we propped a chair under the door handle for extra security before going to bed.

Day 2. *Sunday 4th September.*

Our first Brazilian breakfast was wonderful. A large table in the centre of the dining room was laid out with a magnificent buffet consisting of fresh fruit including mango, melon, pineapple, banana and papaya; an assortment of rolls and sliced bread with butter, ham, cheese, various jams and honey; small squares of cake in various flavours including chocolate, vanilla and coconut; and a selection of fruit juices, tea and coffee.

After the meal, our group met in the hotel foyer where Carol introduced us to our local guide, Giorgio, a tall, slim, serious-looking young man wearing horn-rimmed spectacles. We then boarded the coach waiting outside to take us on a City Tour. Although we had been warned not to take expensive cameras with us, David and I had decided to risk taking our not so expensive camera, hidden in our plastic carrier bag from the local supermarket.

The sky was grey and overcast as we were driven through the underpass we had seen the day before and round Botafogo Bay to the Flamengo area where we stopped to admire the view. Despite the lack of sunshine, the air was warm and bore the scent of freshly cut grass. Before us, across the calm grey waters of the bay, a string of white hotels and tower blocks lined the waterfront, backed by a low green hill behind which rose Sugar Loaf mountain.

This was a lopsided rounded cone of bare striated rock with a small cable car station standing proud at the top. Behind us was the green Parque de Flamengo, its ornamental trees and palms overlooked by tall white apartment blocks, the mountains in the distance deep purple against the threatening skies. The park was being used by cyclists and a few joggers. After taking photographs, we returned to the coach and headed a short way inland to the Gloria area of the city.

Here we stopped to visit the church and monastery of San Sebastian, patron saint of Rio, dating back to 1671. The approach was somewhat uninspiring. From the coach, we walked a short distance to a white concrete building, "like a multi-storey car park," observed Phil, and took a lift up to the fifth floor. As we emerged from the lift, we found that we were at the top of the hill near the entrance to the church which looked deceptively plain on the outside. "Just wait until you see the inside," encouraged Giorgio.

We made our way to the open doors of the church which was packed with Sunday worshippers. 70% of Brazilians are Catholic and those in Rio seemed to be taking their religion very seriously. Mass was taking place and not only were all the pews filled but people were pressed close together down every aisle and were standing squashed about ten deep at the back of the church. Peering over the heads of those standing in the doorway, we could just make out the glorious riot of gold painted baroque carving inside.

In the main body of the church, intricately carved golden pillars were separated by high, ornate golden arches, each with its own balcony above which the pillars rose to form further arches, the airiness of the architecture relieving the heaviness of the decoration. The curved ceiling was comparatively smooth, divided into gold patterned rectangles with oval centres. It was difficult to see from where we were standing in the doorway but above the altar, the ceiling appeared to be covered in paintings. The church was certainly magnificent.

Leaving the worshippers to their devotions, we then walked to the adjacent monastery and Benedictine school for boys which were made of pre-cast concrete and anything but picturesque. Continuing quickly past these, we made our way back to the coach down a steep road which provided views across the harbour.

By this time the skies had cleared and the water was reflecting blue instead of grey, contrasting with the white concrete of the Rio-Niteroi bridge which we could see beyond the harbour. "This is the longest sea bridge in the world, stretching 14 kilometres from shore to shore," declared Giorgio proudly. "That's about nine miles long," said Michael in awe, after a quick calculation. "That's further than my journeys to and from work added together. If you had to walk across that bridge, it would take you about three hours." "It'd be a bit boring," replied Lynne. "I'd rather take the bus. I bet even then it would take twenty minutes to get across." "A lot longer in the rush hour," said her husband.

Once back in the coach, we went to the Centro area, known to the locals as "Downtown". The buildings here are stately and magnificent, dating back to the days when Rio was the capital of Brazil. During the week it is a busy centre of finance and commerce but it is dangerous on a Sunday when businesses are closed and it becomes the haunt of the homeless. We parked beside a large square not far from the former Parliament buildings. Giorgio wanted to show us some old Portuguese houses down a side street on the opposite side of the square and he warned us to leave all our belongings on the coach which would be locked.

As he led us across the square, a group of five young men, sitting beside a central fountain, shouted angrily at us in Portuguese. Our guide shouted back at them equally angrily which seemed to us rather tactless although we obviously had no idea what had been said. As we entered the maze of narrow streets on the opposite side of the square, we were feeling rather apprehensive so we were relieved to find that we were not being followed. However, as we returned to the square, the youths were waiting for us, armed with cobble stones. "They're going to throw those!" David said urgently.

Carol was just assuring him that he was worrying unnecessarily when the first stones came hurtling across at the party. Our official City Guide immediately retaliated by picking up cobble stones himself and hurling them back at the youths while Carol urged us all to make a dash for the coach - we didn't need much persuading.

As we ran, out of the corner of his eye David glimpsed a cobble stone heading straight for his head. He raised his arm for protection and was hit just below the elbow, leaving him in great pain and resulting in a huge purple bruise. Luckily there were no other casualties. The coach driver had remained on board and seeing what was happening, opened the doors as we rushed inside, Giorgio following behind, out of breath and very agitated. The doors closed immediately and as cobble stones crashed against the side of the coach, our driver threw the engine into gear and we sped away. Giorgio apologised and obviously felt very guilty for putting us into such a situation. We decided he must be inexperienced as a tour guide and felt almost sorry for him.

We went a short distance inland to Lapa, passing an impressive double-tiered aqueduct known as the Lapa Arches, and stopped at the modern-looking Cathedral, built in the 1960s. We were glad to be able to purchase bottled water on the Cathedral steps and we sat outside for a few moments, drinking the water and recovering from our recent experience.

When we had relaxed a little, we entered the Cathedral which unlike San Sebastian church was nearly deserted. It is almost conical in shape, with the top of the cone sliced off, and can seat as many as five thousand people in concentric pews round a central altar raised up on a dais. The walls are divided into twelve segments, every third one of which has stained glass windows stretching from floor to ceiling. It reminded me of Coventry Cathedral although it is not at all similar.

From here, we made our way to the foot of Corcovado, famous for its giant statue of Christ the Redeemer standing on the summit, his arms held wide to protect and bless the city below. As we walked from the coach to the cog railway, a group of young men tried to sell us a variety of goods including shuttlecocks and plastic knives. They were very good-humoured and made us laugh with their fooling around. Nobody bought anything but as the train left the station, they chorused cheerfully, "You will come back!"

A young girl aged about 15 had climbed on board with us and, as the train ascended the mountain, she went through the carriages photographing us all despite our protests. The journey uphill was mainly through trees and we only caught occasional glimpses of the views. This was a pity because unfortunately, the cloud was low over the mountain and we alighted from the train into a cold, damp mist. Luckily we had brought waterproof jackets with us which kept out the chill.

We climbed two flights of steps and came to a wide platform. There was a snack bar at the side and the platform was set out with dining tables, each protected by its own opened parasol, now acting as an umbrella. From here, we climbed more steps to the foot of the statue of Christ the Redeemer, over 30 metres high and standing on a high black plinth so that even the base of the statue was several feet above our heads. We were able to gain a sense of its enormous size when a gap in the swirling mist enabled us briefly to make out the whole of the statue, silhouetted grey against the whiter background. There would be spectacular views from this point on a clear day as we knew from the postcards we had seen for sale.

We had been allowed half an hour at the top of Corcovado to include lunch so we returned to the lower platform where we ordered various snacks and sat at the tables under the parasols. David and I each had a bottle of cola and a slice of freshly-cooked pizza, piping hot and absolutely delicious.

As we returned on the train, the young photographer came through the carriages trying to sell the portraits she had taken, each print having been mounted in the centre of a white plastic saucer. She was charging a very high price for each one and refused to reduce it but the photographs were actually very good so despite the extortionate cost, she made a few sales.

Steve and Betty were thrilled with their saucer-portrait. "We'll give it to our daughter in Melbourne as a present," said Steve. We only hoped she would appreciate it. As we left the cog railway, we went back through the ambush of salesmen and boarded our coach again.

Our last visit of the tour was to Sugar Loaf mountain. As we arrived at the base, the skies were clear so we were hoping for good views. The cable car ascended in two stages, the first car taking us to the top of the low green hill we had seen from Flamengo that morning. At this point, the weather was still fine and the summit clear. There was a five minute walk across the plateau of this hill to reach the next cable car station and even from this height, there were stunning views across the island-studded deep blue waters of the bay but Giorgio and Carol hurried us along to the second cable car station so we had little time to take photographs on the way.

As we queued for the next stage of the ascent, Phil suddenly said, "Look, can you see those climbers?" We all peered intently at the mountain until we could make out several coloured dots against the sandy-grey background of the rock. Once we began the ascent in the cable car, we gradually drew closer to the mountain and the dots became larger and clearer until we could distinguish individuals hanging on ropes against the almost sheer sides of the mountain; we could even see some of their movements. Then the clouds began to gather and before we reached the summit the views were blotted out.

Again we were allowed half an hour at the top and as there was a strong wind blowing, we felt confident that the cloud would clear. Those of us with cameras spent most of the time aiming them into the void, each with a finger poised ready to click the shutter. We kept getting a tantalising glimpse of a bay or harbour through the mist but just as we thought it might clear enough for a photograph, the mist thickened from the sea again. It was most frustrating. Back at ground level, we looked up at an almost clear sky apart from a thick ring of cloud encircling the mountain top.

That evening, we were taken to a churrascaria or barbecue, a very popular form of restaurant in Brazil. Having been shown to our tables, we made our way to a buffet where we helped ourselves from a large selection of salads and hot dishes such as rice, white palm shoots and fried banana. We then returned to our seats and waiters brought long skewers, each carrying a particular kind of barbecued meat from which we made our choice, including chunks of pork, beef, lamb, small chicken legs, steak, liver and sausages, all piping hot. Fresh fruit salad and coffee followed and David used his charm to obtain whipped cream for us all, both over the fruit salad and in the coffee, which was much appreciated.

Afterwards, we saw wonderful views of the lights of Rio as we were driven round the coast to one of the Samba Shows for which Rio is famous. We had seats right next to the stage which were perfect for photographs although David's glasses steamed up occasionally during the performance. We were each provided with one free drink and made this last all the evening as we had been warned that extra drinks were very expensive.

The show was very colourful and lively, compèred by a gentleman of African descent dressed in a red suit with white trimmings who strutted about the stage and told jokes in Portuguese. The costumes of the dancers, exactly the same as those worn at Carnival time, were spectacular and completely different for each display.

In one scene, the dancers wore tall red headdresses topped with red ostrich plumes, skimpy sparkling red bikinis, red flounces round the knees and red flounces attached to their hands, extending outwards like wings as the dancers raised their arms.

The New Cathedral

Statue of Christ the Redeemer

Sugar Loaf from the plateau

Samba Show dancers

Leblon Beach, Rio

One of the outfits consisted of a pink and silver round collar and top, joined under the arms, shaped above the bare breasts and linked by a narrow strip of pink and silver down the centre front to a tiny pink bikini bottom embroidered with silver sequins; this was set off by strappy high-heeled pink sandals, pink and silver gloves reaching beyond the elbow, and a pink and silver headdress supporting upright pink ostrich feathers.

One scene featured a woman wearing a sparkling dress in an array of colours with a high neck, long sleeves and very full skirt, hooped out from the hips. She also wore a tall white feather hat and, fastened to her shoulders, an enormous diamond-shaped golden structure sprouting bright yellow feathers. She was accompanied by girls each dressed in a sparkling golden bikini and broad gold armbands, high-heeled gold shoes, a pointed gold dunce's hat decorated with fluffy yellow bobbles, and a golden collar with tall stiff upright points, each topped with a large fluffy yellow bobble supporting a yellow boa, the boas forming a flowing cloak behind.

In another scene, the girls wore dresses of white embroidered satin with layered lacy elbow-length sleeves and long full skirts held out at the bottom by hooped petticoats. From under the lacy layered dress collars hung golden fringed cloaks and on their heads, the girls each wore a shiny white satin turban on which was balanced a pink and silver water jar about two foot high.

There were also male dancers in various satin and tinsel costumes but they played a very minor role in comparison to the girls. At one point, the compère picked on David as he was sitting at the front and persistently urged him to come up on stage. David declined and eventually the compère gave up and managed instead to persuade a

Japanese tourist to come up on stage where he asked him a few questions in English. The tourist was then encouraged to dance with scantily-dressed girls in red tinsel bikinis, a backdrop of feathers and very little else. The man was quite short and the girls towered over him; his head was at breast level which the audience found very amusing. He was a good sport but David curled up with embarrassment for him thinking, "That could be me!"

In between the dancing and posing, we were entertained by a "world-famous" singer of whom none of us had heard but who was very good; a couple dressed in flimsy black who gave a very professional exhibition of Latin-American dancing; five acrobats; and a rope-spinner who used blazing ropes on a darkened stage to great effect. Despite its tackiness and cheap glitz, it was an excellent show. Afterwards, we travelled back to our hotel by coach, giving us another opportunity to admire the lights of Rio de Janeiro.

Day 3. Monday 5th September.

We had a free day in Rio and feeling more confident now, David and I decided to take the camera in our plastic bag again. It was cloudy but bright and we wanted to see a little more of the Botanical Gardens now that we knew which bus to take and where to catch it. On our first visit, we had noticed the Botanical Museum just inside the gates so, having paid for our entrance ticket, we called there first.

As we opened the door and went inside, I saw a notice informing us that the Museum was closed on Mondays. We were just about to leave when a young man who was in the entrance hall at the time introduced himself as the Curator.

He spoke very little English but insisted on opening his Museum just for us and giving us a personally conducted tour. How could we refuse?

He was obviously very proud of the museum which was mainly concerned with the preservation of the Atlantic rainforest. The descriptions above the displays were in Portuguese, Spanish and English and we learned that since the 16th century, the area covered by this coastal rainforest had been reduced to well under 1% of its original size and there were fears that without strict conservation, it would be destroyed completely in the next 10-15 years.

After the tour, the Curator invited us back to his office. "Please, you must take coffee," he insisted. We accepted, feeling we could hardly do otherwise but while we appreciated the invitation, we found it quite difficult to get away without appearing rude. In the end we left, thanking him profusely for his hospitality but making it clear that we had much to see in a limited time.

We enjoyed the Botanical Gardens. We discovered a high level forest walk where we spotted grey squirrels, a humming bird and some beautiful butterflies before descending to the lower levels where we found an ornamental lake. Down one of the avenues, we caught a glimpse of the Statue of Christ the Redeemer on Corcovado. We sat on a bench for a while and chatted to a group of young Mormons from Salt Lake City. They had been sent to Brazil on missionary work and were delighted to be in a city as beautiful as Rio. As before, we were impressed by how quiet, green and peaceful the gardens were, the traffic noise muffled by the shrubs and trees, a haven from the bustle of the city.

By this time, we were feeling hungry. "Let's see if we can find a bus to take us to Leblon," suggested David. "That's the nearest beach area according to the map. There are sure to be some restaurants or hotels round there." The first bus that came along was heading in that direction.

Walking from the bus stop towards the sea, we found a local bar-restaurant situated on a corner with tables set outside on an L-shaped verandah. We sat down and attempted to read the menu but apart from words meaning "chicken" or "fish" we were not much wiser. David approached a gentleman in a business suit seated at the next table. "Excuse me", he said, "I wonder if you would help us please."

The man was very friendly and did his best to translate for us but had difficulty in trying to describe the dishes in English so we placed our orders hopefully, uncertain of what we would receive. After a short wait, David was served with a kind of beef stew with triangular potato chips while I was given what turned out to be chicken and cheese in a batter with rice and mashed potato. We tried each other's dishes and approved.

After the meal, we wandered the short distance to the seafront and saw to our right a headland on which stood the Sheraton Hotel. "Let's walk up there a little way," I suggested. "We should get a good view back across the bay to Leblon Beach." It turned out to be an excellent view. Checking that nobody was standing too close, we brought out the camera for a quick photograph before returning it to the plastic bag. A group of surfers were making the most of the almost non-existent waves so we decided to walk back to the beach to watch them for a while.

"We ought to have a paddle while we're here." We took off our shoes and socks, rolled up our trouser legs and made our way down the sandy beach and into the water. Despite the warmth of the sun, the sea was cold enough to make us gasp so after only a few moments hopping from one leg to the other, we made our way back to the sea wall, dried our feet and warmed them in the sun before putting our socks and shoes on again. We then started walking back to our hotel along the length of Leblon, Ipanema and Copacabana Beaches, a distance of three or four miles, keeping to the pavement which made walking easier.

At intervals we passed stalls selling coconut milk. When we came to the first stall, David said, "I haven't had fresh coconut milk for years." I thought back. "I don't think I've ever tasted it." Seats and tables with parasols were provided so we sat down and ordered a drink. The stallholder selected two fresh coconuts from the top of the pile and slicing off the tops, passed them to us with a straw each. The milk was watery and sweet with a delicate flavour, very refreshing.

School football teams were practising at intervals along the beach and we stopped to watch some of these. "That looks hard work," I commented, watching how the soft sand deadened the movement of the ball. "There's some impressive footwork," approved my husband, a keen football fan. "I wouldn't be surprised to see some of them playing in the World Cup at some time in the future."

The pavement on which we were walking was decorated in traditional Portuguese black and white mosaic patterns. We passed one part where workmen were carrying out repairs. Carefully removing the small black and white stones, they mixed and laid small amounts of concrete and then laboriously fitted the stones back into the original pattern like a jigsaw puzzle. It took a great deal of time and patience and we concluded that either wages must be very low or the council very rich (or both) to afford the cost.

Halfway along Ipanema Beach, we came to the Caesar Park Hotel which was advertising its rooftop coffee bar. "I wouldn't mind seeing the view from up there," I said. "Do you feel ready for another drink yet?" We went inside and took a lift up to the 23rd floor where tables and chairs were arranged in the open air around a swimming pool. The area was surrounded by glass screens through which were lovely views along the coast in both directions and we sat drinking cool, freshly-squeezed orange juice and resting our feet.

From here, we cut inland to the Avenue Nossa Senhora de Copacabana, a shopping street at the southern end of Copacabana Beach. The shops that looked so interesting from the bus were less attractive when we walked past them and could have been in a city anywhere in the world. Darkness was now beginning to fall and as we were still a mile or so from the hotel, we caught a bus back to Leme. That evening after a meal with the group, we went for a short walk along the seafront for a last look at the lights before returning to our room and packing our cases.

2

THE PANTANAL

Day 4. Tuesday 6th September.

We were woken at 4am to be ready to leave an hour later. We staggered bleary-eyed into the dining room, hoping for a cup of coffee to bring us round and found that, even at that unearthly hour, we were served with the full Brazilian breakfast including the cake selection. "I don't really feel hungry," I mumbled. "You'd better eat something, you don't know when you'll get your next meal," said my husband, filling his plate.

We set off for the airport before dawn and on the way, were surprised to see youngsters already practising their football on the floodlit pitches. Talk about enthusiastic!

We checked in at the airport without any problems. As I waited in the Departure Lounge, still half-asleep, my gaze wandered for a moment; then I looked down at the rucksack beside my feet and to my horror, it was no longer there. "Don't panic!" I told myself firmly, my heart thumping, and without moving from the spot, I looked around. Then I saw Karl, James and Graham standing together grinning at me and Karl pulled my rucksack out from behind them. "That got you going!" laughed James. "Don't forget to watch your luggage!" Karl admonished as he handed it over. It was a most effective way of drumming home the message. Whenever I put my rucksack down after that, I made sure I had my foot through the strap.

We enjoyed the low level flight from Rio de Janeiro to Belo Horizonte over an undulating sea of red-brown soil, splashed with vivid patches of greens and golds from newly emerging crops and dotted with the occasional hacienda and even more occasional town. We stopped in Belo Horizonte for about fifteen minutes to allow passengers to disembark and new passengers to come on board before continuing to our destination, Cuiabá, situated in the Mato Grosso region of Brazil.

Again we kept at an altitude low enough to see the scenery. Particularly striking were large green segmented circular fields of irrigated crops scattered across the landscape; they looked exactly like enormous versions of the pie charts used in company reports.

As we alighted from the aircraft in Cuiabá, we were immediately struck by the heat. While temperatures in Rio had been a pleasant 20-25° Centigrade or mid-70° s Fahrenheit with a cooling breeze, here in Cuiabá it was in the mid-30°s Centigrade or about 90° Fahrenheit - it was **hot**! Carol told us briefly that Cuiabá was developed after gold was discovered nearby at the start of the 18th century and that it was at one time the capital of the Mato Grosso. From here, we were heading south into the Pantanal.

The ancient bus waiting for us outside the airport was very narrow with no storage space for the luggage. "Right, men," said Graham. "It looks like we need to load all the cases on to the back seats." While Phil and Karl climbed into the bus to pack the cases inside, the rest of the men in the party made a human chain and the luggage was soon loaded via the rear window. We then took our seats; there were just enough left to go round.

We had to hold our hand luggage as there was insufficient room to put it on the floor by our feet. There was no glass in the windows so once we set off, the bus was pleasantly air-conditioned; however, after about an hour's driving the tarmac road gave way to a dirt track so it became extremely dusty.

After about three hours on the road, we came to a small shop-cum-post office with toilets where we had a welcome break for fifteen minutes. This being the only shop for miles around, it stocked a strange assortment of necessities such as flour, household utensils and medicines, plus hats and postcards for the tourists. On the counter were a few home-made spicy meatballs and packets of crisps and there was a small refrigerator containing ices. I was beginning to feel hungry. "I'm going to try one of those meatballs. Would you like one?" David declined so I bought one for myself and found it very tasty. Most of the others bought ice-creams which seemed a good idea in view of the heat so David chose a choc-ice while I selected plain vanilla. We all stocked up with bottled water as we had been told there would be nowhere else to buy any for the next three days.

We were very glad that we had eaten something when, some time after we had left, it dawned on us that this had been the lunch stop. However, we had already been offered three consecutive breakfasts that morning, one at the hotel in Rio, one on the flight to Belo Horizonte and a third on the flight to Cuiabá, so none of us was exactly starving. About an hour later, we came to a rustic wooden sign painted red with white lettering suspended from a wooden beam about ten feet above the road. This sign proclaimed that we were on the Transpantaneira which, Carol told us, was a highway originally planned to connect Cuiabá to Corumbá, a distance of about 300 kilometres. "The Government ran out of money and had to abandon the project at about the halfway mark," she said. On either end of the beam hung a smaller wooden sign stating "Here beginning the Pantanal. Welcome."

As we entered the Pantanal, Carol explained that this huge area of swampland extends across the borders into Brazil, Bolivia and Paraguay and is drained by the River Paraguai and its tributaries. "There are just two seasons, wet and dry," she told us. "In the rainy season, from October to March, the rivers overflow their banks and flood most of the area. During this period, the water can rise by up to ten feet and you can see fish swimming through the branches of the trees while the animals are left crowded together on small islands of dry land. I've been told," she added, "that the prettiest time is in January when nearly all the trees and shrubs are in flower. Unfortunately, this is also the time when the malaria carrying mosquitoes are out in full force so very few visitors ever see the Pantanal in all its glory."

Being September, we were there towards the end of the dry season when the mosquitoes had retreated, the rivers had receded and the floods had shrunk to small pools on either side of the raised-up highway. Even at this time of the year, the Pantanal was still very green and many of the trees were covered in beautiful bright pink or yellow blossoms.

The pools of water were teeming with fish that had been condensed into smaller and smaller areas and jacarés (the local alligators) were plentiful along the banks.

We stopped by one pool where two boys were fishing. One was sitting perched on a narrow plank of wood that stretched out into the water and he was catching fish with a small net while the other was taking each fish as it was caught and stringing it on to a line which already held nearly twenty fish.

We were just wondering whether the fish were for sale or home consumption when we were distracted by a rumble of hooves and a cloud of dust rose in the distance; a large herd of cattle was being driven along the highway from one of the vast haciendas. "On board, on board," urged our driver, naturally reluctant to let them overtake us. Some of the party climbed back into the bus but James said to Carol, "Can I just hang on until they come a little closer so I can take a photo?" I also wanted to get a shot of some real cowboys so we waited as long as possible, until they were only about thirty yards away.

The cattle were led by three men sitting confidently astride their horses and all wearing wide-brimmed hats and short sleeved shirts and carrying long wooden poles. Behind them followed the herd, crushed tightly together across the full width of the raised up highway. These were white zebu cattle with long slender legs, humped backs, long narrow faces, floppy ears and horns curving above their heads like crescent moons. Once we were back on the coach, Carol told us that despite the seasonal flooding, ranching is very important to the local economy. "It's compatible with the wildlife," she assured us, "as very few other animals feed upon the same grasses as the cattle."

We continued along the Transpantaneira for another hour passing only a few scattered haciendas and petrol stations until we turned off to the left, on to a gated road. We stopped while the driver went to a nearby house for the key to the gate. "Carol, what are those?" asked Mary, pointing up into a tree just to the right of the bus. Following her directions, we saw some very tiny green birds like budgerigars briefly emerging from the centre of a large untidy twiggy nest hanging from the tree and Carol told us they were parakeets. Then our driver returned, opened the gate and we continued on our way.

Having followed a narrow single track road for a distance of about four kilometres, the bus stopped just outside the entrance to the compound where we were to spend the next three nights. We unloaded the luggage as quickly as possible and carried it inside where we were met by Katarina and Beder, the owners of the property, who welcomed us and showed us to our accommodation.

We were staying in small brick bungalows with tiled roofs, constructed near the entrance to the compound. Each bungalow was divided into four bedrooms, two at the front and two at the rear. Outside each bedroom was a concrete verandah with a wooden chair and a hammock suspended from the wall to a corner beam while inside were twin beds built of brick, each with a mattress on top, and a wooden wardrobe with fitted shelves. We also had a separate shower room and toilet with running water while electricity was provided by a generator. All the comforts of civilisation!

The windows had no glass but were covered in mosquito netting and there was a wooden shutter which could be closed over the bedroom window to give privacy at night, although we noted with surprise that there was no such privacy in the shower, which had a large netted window.

As soon as we had put our bags in our rooms, Katarina and Beder invited us all to meet at the bar for a welcoming drink. The bar and restaurant were about a hundred yards away, at the opposite end of the dry dusty compound. There were plenty of trees giving welcome shade and a scattering of fallen leaves lay among exposed tree roots on the bare ground. Running alongside the compound on the left was a river about thirty foot wide, green with water hyacinth and, we were to discover, swarming with piranha fish and jacarés.

Katarina and Beder had semi-tamed three jacarés by feeding them daily but they warned us not to get too close. "You're reasonably safe if you approach them from the side because they take time to turn round," Beder told us, "but if you walk in front of them, they have a frightening turn of speed."

We had no intentions of experimenting as these alligators were particularly vicious looking creatures with curved jaws that gave the appearance of a permanent evil grin and with very long pointed teeth, those from their upper jaws hanging down outside their mouths and those from their lower jaws sticking up through holes in their nostrils.

After being given a quick tour of the compound, we had time to freshen up and relax for a while before meeting at the bar again, prior to the evening meal. "I feel really dirty after that journey," said David. "I think I'll have a shower." "That's a good idea," I agreed. "We don't need the light on at the moment so the mosquito netting will give us some privacy."

David went into the shower room first, laughed out loud and called me in. "Look at these," he said and showed me three tiny tree frogs which had taken up residence near the taps. They were flattened green creatures little more than an inch in length, very tame and full of curiosity. We soon discovered that when we went into the shower and turned on the taps, they would scurry up the wall and across to the wooden batten which held the top of the mosquito netting in place. They would then sit there in the dry, peering down at us from over the edge of the batten. We became quite fond of them during the few days we were there.

By the time we made our way back to the bar, it was already dark and we discovered why we had been asked to bring torches with us on holiday. Not only did we have to negotiate our way over rough, unknown ground and look out for jacarés, snakes and other creepy-crawlies on the way, but we also had to avoid a large empty pit, lined with concrete and about four foot deep which could have caused a great deal of damage had we fallen into it. As we crossed the compound, we flashed the torchlight from side to side in a wide arc to ensure that there was nothing nasty around.

We had smothered all our exposed skin in insect repellent before leaving our room which was just as well because the tables and chairs beside the bar were out in the open on a raised wooden platform and although it was the low season for malaria mosquitoes, I have the type of skin which attracts any kind of biting insect.

We all bought drinks and David had a guava juice while I chose mango; passion fruit juice later became my favourite. The drinks were quite expensive but understandably so as they had to be brought such a distance.

While we waited for Katarina to let us know when the meal was ready, we all sat and chatted and soon discovered that most of the others also had frogs in the shower. Shelagh was disappointed that she had no wildlife in her accommodation so we promised she could come and see ours. When Katarina called to us, we walked across the small wooden bridge connecting the bar platform to the restaurant and in through the light mesh door with its bamboo frame.

The restaurant was circular with wooden walls up to a height of about three feet. The walls above this consisted of mosquito netting stretched between tall wooden uprights and there was a circular fan in the centre of the bamboo ceiling.

Pantanal cattle ranchers

River beside the compound

Early morning in the Pantanal

Jacaré

The circular table was large enough to take all seventeen of us and Katarina and her helpers provided us with a wonderful three course evening meal consisting of a vegetable soup with home-made bread, tender stewed beef with vegetables and rice followed by fresh fruit salad.

After the meal Katarina and Beder warned us that under no circumstances were we to leave the compound between dusk and dawn unless accompanied by one of their men who would be carrying a weapon. During the day we could walk outside but even then we should never venture out alone.

"Only a few weeks ago, in broad daylight," cautioned Beder, "a visitor went just a few yards beyond the entrance to the compound by himself. He saw a jaguar watching him from across the nearest pool of water beside the track and as he was close to the compound, he turned and ran back inside. It can be dangerous here at any time."

After the meal, David and I stood outside near the bar, chatting to the four Australians. I felt an itching round my ankles which I tried to ignore but eventually I had to say to them, "Please excuse me, I think I'm being bitten. I need to go back to the room." As we only had one torch between us, David came with me. Once inside, we shut the door, put the light on and I peeled down my ankle socks.

Although I had put insect repellent on my legs down to sock level, I hadn't realised that sandflies could penetrate through socks without difficulty and in the short time we had stood talking, I had acquired fifty-seven bites round my ankles. Despite rubbing in plenty of anti-histamine cream, the itching was almost unbearable for the next day or two. I didn't make that mistake again.

Day 5. Wednesday 7th September.

Our guide, Carlos, knocked on all our doors to wake us at 5am to prepare for a walk starting just before dawn. As we were about to leave the compound, we heard a ferocious roaring in the distance. "Are those jaguars?" asked Mary nervously. "No, don't worry," Carlos reassured her. "It's only a troupe of howler monkeys. You often hear them at this time of day." Then, putting his forefinger to his lips, he whispered "Please remain silent."

Carlos led us through the darkness down the track along which we had been driven the previous afternoon. At first nobody spoke as we peered into the blackness on either side of the track, searching for even blacker silhouettes. After a time however, as nothing moved, people began whispering to each other and then, little by little, to talk more loudly.

The sky gradually lightened and then the sun rose, small and dull red in the morning mist. In places the track was bordered by shrubs, three to four foot high, bearing large convolvulus-like flowers with pale pink, delicately fluted edges and a deep pink centre. These shrubs made it difficult to look for animals as they hid the waterholes on either side of the track.

With the dawn came a wealth of bird life particularly herons, egrets and enormous red-collared Jabiru storks, known locally as tuiuíu (pronounced too-yoo-**yoo**). One flew past us, its vulture-like head and sunken neck making it look prehistoric and its wingspan appearing to be at least five feet across. "Wow," breathed Phil in awe. "Pterodactyl!" Carlos told us that the Jabirus are among the largest flying birds in the western hemisphere. As the sun rose higher and the mist cleared, fewer birds were to be seen although we spotted a pair of toucans in a distant tree, easily recognisable by their huge yellow bills. "You're very lucky," said Carlos. "Toucans are rare in this area." We also saw the dangling nests of weaver birds although there was no sign of occupancy.

Beside the path rose grey, pitted termite mounds, two to three feet high, while next to every small pool of water, jacarés stretched their necks, raising their toothy jaws as if sniffing the morning air. Carlos stopped us beside one waterhole and pointed to where the trunk of a young tree grew out of the water. "Look," he said, "can you see that snake down there, just below water level? That's an anaconda. It can grow to as long as twenty five feet and coils round its victims before crushing them to death." Wrapped around the trunk, we could just make out the thick golden coils of the snake. "Please don't disturb it," added Carlos, rather unnecessarily.

Throughout the walk we were accompanied by the sound of very quarrelsome birds which we never saw as they were well hidden in the undergrowth, the first ones questioning in four rising notes, the others responding with four falling notes, (diddle-e-**dee**? **diddle**-e-doh! diddle-e-**dee**? **diddle**-e-doh!) reminding us of a group of cheerleaders.

At 7.30am we returned to the compound with an appetite for breakfast. This consisted of tea or coffee, home-made bread, butter and honey, papaya slices, little sweet biscuits and small savoury pastries containing pieces of ham. In daylight, we could see through the mosquito netting and the restaurant became a shelter for observing wild-life. Not far from the dining area lay hollowed out logs which Katarina had filled with scraps to attract the birds; they also attracted the alligators.

We had a morning to relax, watching tree lizards and jacarés in the compound or lying in the hammock, reading or listening to the birds, whistling and whooping overhead.

One bird had a particularly piercing two-tone whistle; "pee-wee, pee-wee" it called, the sound echoing through the trees to a background chorus of cicadas.

After lunch, we were split into two groups. The other group were taken piranha fishing while those in our group were given the choice of going into the bush by horse and cart, by bicycle or on horseback. As David and I had never ridden a horse in our lives, a shortcoming we have since rectified, and neither of us had ridden a bicycle since we were at school, we opted for the cart which we shared with Betty. Jack and Jean were both experienced equestrians and chose the horses while everyone else elected to ride bicycles.

As we left the compound, our guide led us almost immediately off the main track on to a side path. Our horse had only gone a few yards when he decided he had had enough and tried to turn back, reversing the cart into the bushes in the process and filling our hair with twigs and insects. "Oh no," squealed Betty. "I **hate** spiders" and laughing, we all shook our hair and brushed our shoulders clear as our driver climbed down to lead the horse which, for some reason, was still very unwilling. Half in hope, half fear, David said, "Do you think he can scent danger? There may be a jaguar about."

The track led across several wooden bridges which made all the horses very nervous. As the bridges were made up of several layers of wooden planks laid across each other, we thought perhaps they could sense that, below the top layer, the planks were rotted through. Jack and Jean found that they had to dismount from their horses at each bridge and lead the animals across.

Our horse refused point blank to cross the first bridge we came to. Instead, it careered down the steep bank, ignoring the efforts of our driver who was still valiantly trying to lead it, dragging him along and nearly tipping the cart over in the process. David, Betty and I clung on tightly to the sides of the cart, expecting to be thrown out at any moment. The horse then took us across the river bed which luckily had nearly dried up at this point.

After this near-accident, the three of us decided not to take any further chances so we climbed out of the cart whenever we approached another bridge, which was every few yards. The cyclists had the toughest time as their tyres sank into the sandy track and with the heat, they were soon exhausted.

After a couple of miles, we all dismounted, the horses were tied up and Carlos, our guide, led us off the path into the bush, warning us to stay silent. Although none of us uttered a word, the noise of eight people crashing through dead branches half hidden by the undergrowth must have scared away any wildlife for miles around.

We made our way to the river but were not surprised when we saw neither birds nor animals; however, the flowers were very pretty. Apart from white water hyacinths, the edges of their petals tinged with purple, I saw a wild amaryllis sporting half a dozen red-orange trumpets with lemon-green centres and we passed several trees covered in clouds of vivid yellow or pink blossoms. We then returned to the compound on our various forms of transport.

Although our horse was now on his way back, he still only seemed happy when he was behind the cyclists, presumably working on the theory that if they were not attacked and the bridges held up under their weight, it was reasonably safe for him to follow. By the time we were back inside the compound, the cyclists were absolutely exhausted. Lynne had doubted whether she would make it but she did and immediately collapsed in her hammock, her face glowing bright red with heat and exertion.

After a short rest, those who wished had the opportunity to go out on a trailer behind the jeep to see what wildlife they could spot at dusk. Most of the cyclists decided they were too tired but the rest of the party left the compound at 4pm and we bounced our way along the track to the Transpantaneira Highway in the open trailer on which were three bench seats, one behind the other, each wide enough to seat four people. It felt so different from being enclosed in a coach; there was a real sense of freedom and being close to nature.

On this part of the trip, all we saw were jacarés and, as we were joining the main road, some of the little green parakeets leaving the nest near the entrance gate. Then, as we drove down the Highway and the light began to fade, we started to see hawks, black and white kingfishers, storks and herons. Later still, we caught sight of two toucans on a tree in the distance, some macaws flew overhead and we excitedly spotted a flock of pink spoonbills in a nearby field.

As dusk fell, a family of capybara, two adults and two young, crossed a clearing before disappearing into the bush. Carlos told us that capybara are the largest rodents in the world and spend much of the day in water to keep cool, coming out in the evening to feed on the vegetation. By now we were really thrilled with what we had seen and completely satisfied with our outing.

We were making our way back to the compound and it was nearly dark when Carlos pointed out two spider monkeys which we could just about glimpse as dark shapes in the overhanging branches of a tree and then two more capybara, little more than black outlines against the darkness, crossed the road in front of us. Wonderful!

Horse riders

Following the cyclists

Jabiru nest

Evening trailer ride

Later, as we sat at the bar before dinner, the most enormous toad, a yellow-beige in colour, climbed on to the walkway to the dining room and sat there, giving us all plenty of opportunity to observe it. It must have been at least eight inches in length and seemed completely unfazed by the attention it was getting. "Don't go away," I said to it, "I'm just going to fetch my camera from the bedroom." Unfortunately, by the time I returned, the toad had vanished. Nonetheless, it was a very satisfying evening!

Day 6. Thursday 8th September.

David and I woke early and were out by 5.30am again. As we made our way to the edge of the compound, we saw Shelagh standing at the entrance. "Did you hear that sound?" she asked nervously as we came up to her. We listened and heard a kind of coughing noise. "I think that might be a jaguar. Do you reckon we're safe?" she queried. We also thought it might be a big cat but the three of us decided to venture out together. "There are plenty of pebbles on the path," said David bravely. "I'm sure that if we all shout loudly and throw stones, it'll be enough to scare any jaguar away."

We kept our eyes skinned and remained silent as we walked down the track and we were fortunate enough to see a river otter crossing the path just in front of us on its way from one pool to another. There were fewer birds than on the previous morning but we managed to come quite close to a huge Jabiru stork that took off and passed only inches above our heads. "Hey," breathed Shelagh, instinctively ducking, "that's neat!"

After breakfast, a morning walk was arranged but it was very hot and David and I thought it would be an unprofitable exercise. Instead, we decided to spend the morning around the compound, seeing what we could spot without the effort of walking. This proved much more rewarding.

Katarina had three large tortoises that she kept as pets and we watched her feeding these while she told us in broken English and sign language how she and Beder had met in Caracas where she had been studying and how it had been love at first sight. We watched a large number of lizards of varying sizes running up and down the trees in the compound and then a dragon-like monitor lizard, nearly four feet in length and banded in spotted grey and white came out of the bush and slowly made its way down to the river to drink, its red forked tongue continually flickering in and out. We gazed, fascinated, until it climbed the bank again and vanished back into the bush.

The birds were beautiful particularly the golden orioles, flashing bright golden yellow as they flew between the trees, and the yellow-billed cardinals, each about the size of a wagtail, with pure white breast and underside, scarlet head, yellow beak and slate-grey wings. Jacanas, otherwise known as lily-trotters, scuttled across the water hyacinths, showing off their long legs and large-toed feet, rusty-orange bodies, black heads and necks and orange-yellow beaks.

In the back of one of the canoes stood a very large, handsome and seemingly tame red bittern, waiting to pounce on any passing fish. He must have been about three feet high with long sturdy legs, a large slate-grey pointed beak, a reddish-brown head and upper back, snow-white breast with a centre red-brown stripe like a tie worn over a white shirt, and dove-grey wings and tail. Katarina saw us watching him, led us to the centre of the compound and pointed up into one of the trees, saying, "Home, home". We peered up through the branches but we were unable to spot the nest.

When the party returned, they looked hot and tired. They had seen no wildlife but they said they had enjoyed the walk. For lunch that day we had pacu, a fish that swims under the trees to feed on ripe fruit as it drops into the river. This fish had the most wonderful gleaming white teeth like a set of human dentures but it was very tough and chewy to eat.

After lunch, the party split up again and it was our turn to go piranha fishing. We watched the others depart on bicycles, on horseback and in the cart and relaxed until mid-afternoon. Then three of the men from the compound, carrying home-made fishing rods and bait, took us along narrow paths through the forest for about half a mile. Two walked in front of us and one brought up the rear, all armed with knives and rifles in case of an emergency. The fact that this was considered necessary gave us a frisson of excitement.

When we reached the river, three canoes were waiting for us, each man being responsible for paddling one of the canoes. David, Shelagh and I shared one canoe but found that when it came to fishing, we had drawn the short straw as our man, Marco, had only kept one fishing rod for us to share between us. These fishing rods were home-made affairs consisting of a length of string with a hook on one end, the other end tied to a four foot bamboo cane. The men had chopped up some fish caught the previous day to use as bait and luckily we had plenty of this so we took it in turns to fasten a piece of fish to the hook and lower it into the water.

The three canoes were spread out across the river and our friends in the other canoes, who had a fishing rod each, started getting bites almost immediately but not us! For a start, Marco had paddled the canoe in among the water hyacinths which kept getting caught on the hook while the other canoes were in open water. Eventually he realised there was a problem, paddled us into a stretch of clear river and we began to get bites.

We were not very skilled at piranha fishing. Most of the time, the piranhas nibbled the bait so gently that it was gone before we knew they were there. When it was my turn, I did manage to lift two out of the water but they let go and fell back into the river before I could get them on board. David and Shelagh were not even that successful. Those in the other two canoes did rather better and caught six piranhas between them. These piranhas were quite small, less than four inches in length, and a lovely golden colour with small sharp pointed teeth like fretsaw blades.

That evening, Beder told us that once they have been caught, piranhas cause more injuries in canoes, particularly to barefoot Indians, than they do to people swimming in the rivers. Carol later told us that the Indians hang piranha jaws on their necklaces and use them for cutting their hair.

When the bait had run out, the men paddled us back down the river to the compound. In places, the weed was so thick that it looked almost impenetrable and we wondered what would happen if we were tipped out among the piranhas and jacarés. We had been told that there were many different kinds of piranha, several kinds being vegetarian, but judging from the enthusiasm with which these had removed the bait from our hooks, we concluded that we were definitely surrounded by the meat eating varieties.

The wooden seats were very hard and I wished I had a cushion. "I'm stiff," I complained, wriggling slightly and the canoe tilted alarmingly. "Hey, stop fidgeting," said

David, sounding worried. I tried to shift my weight very gently, first to one side and then the other. Shelagh and David were also suffering from aches and pains but, despite our discomfort, it was a thoroughly enjoyable trip and we were sorry when it was over.

As the canoe pulled in to shore, two jacarés came rushing down the bank to greet us, like pet dogs coming to welcome us home. "Go, quick!" ordered Marco. Luckily, the jacarés were both approaching from the same side so we hopped out of the canoe on the other side and ran up the bank as quickly as our stiff legs would allow while Marco paddled back into the river to moor further along the bank where it was clear.

When we arrived back in our room, we heard an angry buzzing noise coming from an enormous insect trying unsuccessfully to escape through the mosquito netting covering our window. "Let's get rid of it," I said, with some trepidation, looking around for something large enough in which to catch it. The insect bore a slight resemblance to a dragonfly, about three inches long, but with a bright turquoise triangle hanging downwards at the tip of its tail which was eye-catching and looked dangerous.

While David stood holding the door open, I put a drinking glass at an angle in front of the insect and gently pushed it inside with a postcard which I then held underneath to prevent it escaping. I carried it outside, shook the insect free and ran back into the room in case it attacked; luckily it was only too pleased to fly away.

That night there was an optional evening walk into the bush. We thought once again that if large numbers were going, there would be little to see so we opted out and did our packing instead. When the rest of the group returned, James and Phil enthusiastically told us how exciting it had been, finding their way in the dark. Also, Carlos had captured a baby jacaré by the river bank; he had found it when its eyes glowed red in the torchlight.

Day 7. Friday 9th September.

As this was our last opportunity, David and I arranged to meet Shelagh at the entrance to the compound just before dawn. We didn't spot any animals on our walk on this occasion although we heard the howler monkeys roaring in the distance. To make up for this, however, we saw plenty of herons, storks and egrets. We had previously noticed a Jabiru stork's nest which had appeared to be deserted, high in a tree, not far from the entrance to the compound; on this occasion, however, the adult stork was feeding two young ones.

We returned early to finish off last minute packing before breakfast. Back in our room, I felt my hip itching and on investigation, found a small tick. "Ugh!" I shuddered and without thinking, I pulled it off and dropped it into the toilet. David was horrified and insisted that we both stripped and inspected each other in case we had picked up any more. Afterwards I remembered that you should never pull a tick off your skin in case it has its head under the surface; this head might then break off and turn septic. Luckily I suffered no ill effects from my hasty action and the skin soon healed. We found no further ticks.

Breakfast that morning consisted of tea or coffee, papaya and melon slices, chocolate cake and chicken and vegetable pie. While we were eating, some agoutis came out of the forest to feed from the hollowed-out logs, sitting back on their haunches and using their front paws to put the food into their mouths.

All too soon it was time to leave. We bade a reluctant farewell to Katarina, Beder and the men who waved to us as we set off down the track to the Transpantaneira Highway. Carlos was coming with us as far as the airport. By the time we reached the main road, the temperature was rising rapidly and hundreds of alligators were warming themselves on the banks.

As we stopped to take photographs, we found it hard to appreciate that their numbers are threatened by poachers who kill possibly thousands every week. "The poachers only strip a small piece of skin from the flanks of each animal and throw the rest of the carcass away for the scavengers to eat," Carlos explained. "Most of the skins find their way to North America to make shoes, belts and handbags. As long as people continue to buy these goods, it will be impossible to protect the jacarés."

We found that even on the Transpantaneira Highway, the bridges were rather dodgy. We were on a larger coach than the one we had used from Cuiabá and on this trip, we were all asked to get off the coach and walk across each bridge to reduce the load. Some bridges were visibly rotting while most had huge nails sticking up at the sides where they had worked loose. Two rows of double planks, a vehicle width apart, had been laid lengthwise across the horizontal timbers of each bridge and the car, coach and lorry drivers all tried to line up their vehicles so that the tyres ran along these lengthwise planks as they crossed the bridges. Fortunately, although this is the only road through this part of the Pantanal, there was comparatively little traffic using it.

We were on our way back to the airport at Cuiabá but as we had plenty of time to spare, Carol arranged a detour to Poconé, a prosperous little town with paved streets, a tarmac road and an enormous cathedral. This town had made its wealth from a gold mine which we were to visit. When we arrived, we stood at the top of the quarry and gazed down towards a muddy orange lake at the bottom.

The soil looked predominantly light beige and sandy yellow in colour tinged with pink and grey and full of rocks and shale. Mechanical diggers were tearing it away in chunks and loading it into huge hoppers. The hopper contents were then taken to be crushed and washed to obtain any gold-dust residue. "I wouldn't mind spending some time here looking for gold," said Karl. Unfortunately, however, panning for gold was not an option. As we drove back through the town, we passed schools, a hospital and a large sports arena. The community is obviously reaping benefits from the mine.

A short distance from Poconé, our driver noticed a strange phenomenon in the sky and stopped the coach so we could all get out to have a look. "Make sure you're wearing your sunglasses," warned Carol. The sun was encircled by a large ring of light with another circle of light overlapping it. Carlos said it was an eclipse but the sun was not shadowed in any way.

We arrived at Cuiabá airport at 1pm with two and a half hours to find lunch. David and I wandered round a built up square outside the airport entrance and at the far end, we found a pleasant little restaurant with tables outside in the shade and samba music playing over a loudspeaker.

At the other end of the restaurant courtyard was a small wooden shelter with open walls and a partly tiled roof. Four loudly squawking macaws were climbing over and under the roof beams; two were blue and yellow, two were red and green. We walked across and David starting talking to the two nearest birds. The other two immediately became jealous and started pecking at the first two macaws and jostling to be the centre of attention. After taking their photographs, we returned to our table and ordered a meal each.

Further down the courtyard, we noticed James, Phil, Graham, Karl and Nigel sharing a table together. They had ordered a large pizza between them and when it was served, came over to us in a group carrying two large slices. "Would you like some of our pizza?" asked Graham, "It's too much for us to manage." As we had already placed our order, we thanked them but declined.

The men hung around for a little while making small talk so, as there were only two spare seats at our table and those on either side were occupied, we asked if they would like us to move down the restaurant to a table next to theirs. "Well actually," James confessed sheepishly, "the real reason we came over to chat to you was to have a closer look at that gorgeous girl on the next table." A slim, attractive young Brazilian girl with dark eyes and long dark wavy hair was sitting at the table behind us with an older companion.

At that moment, our own meal arrived and our friends reluctantly made their way back to their own table where their pizza was getting cold. David has the happy knack of being able to communicate with anyone and despite being unable to speak more than a few words of Portuguese, started chatting to the Brazilian couple. Having first obtained permission, we then embarrassed James by calling him over and introducing him to the dark-haired beauty.

He blushingly asked if he might have a photograph of the two of them together and was amazed and delighted when she grabbed him by the hand and led him over to some flowering shrubs that would make an attractive background. Using James' new camera, I took a snapshot of them, keeping my fingers crossed that it turned out all right.

After a leisurely meal, we then slowly made our way back to the coach which was waiting outside the airport, collected our luggage and checked in for the flight to our next destination, Salvador de Bahia.

3

Salvador de Bahia

It was dark when we arrived in Salvador which, Carol had warned us, was even more dangerous than Rio. Our party left the airport in three vans, the drivers of which insisted on travelling in convoy and going at full speed straight through all the red traffic lights, convincing us that had they stopped, we would have been mugged and had all our luggage stolen.

We reached the hotel at 11pm and as soon as we had the key, went straight up to our room on the third floor. "It smells very musty," I said as I opened the door, "and it's a bit hot and airless in here." "Well, the air conditioning's on," David pointed out. "Listen to the racket it's making." A very ancient, rusty looking box up at ceiling level was rattling very loudly and seemingly ineffectually. We managed to open the window which let in some fume-laden air and the noise of traffic from the busy main road outside.

David went into the bathroom and "Oh, **dar**ling!" he exclaimed. "What is it?" I asked, beginning to undo the suitcases. He came out almost immediately looking disgusted. "It looks as though someone's cut himself

59

shaving and it's never been cleaned up," he said. "There's blood all over the mirror and the wall behind it."

I followed him back into the bathroom where we also found blood spattered on the wall behind the toilet and down beside the washbasin. Investigating further, we found bloodstains in the bedroom near the skirting board and in the corridor just outside our room; there was also blood spattered dull red down the outside of the grey lift door.

We decided an attempted murder had taken place there very recently and we imagined the injured man crawling from the bathroom to the lift to seek help. We went down to Reception and complained. "It's only red paint," the receptionist assured us. "It was spilt accidentally. In any case, it's nearly midnight, there's nothing we can do at this time of night."

We had seen nothing painted red anywhere so we were totally unconvinced. However, the receptionist promised to find us another room the next day and we had no alternative but to return to our room. We left the window open to try to get rid of the smell but we had very little sleep that night. A crowd clapping and singing outside at 2 o'clock in the morning didn't help.

Day 8. Saturday 10th September.

We were up at 6am for breakfast which, incidentally, was excellent. Immediately after the meal, we were introduced to Bernardo, our guide, and set off at 7am on a city tour. First we walked a short distance to Independence Square which took its name following independence from the Portuguese in 1760.

In the centre of the square was a white plinth carrying a tall fluted grey column with the statue of a heroic figure on top; the plinth was surrounded by four smaller white columns, each with its own grey statue and between the columns on the nearest sides were a stone eagle and lion. Paths radiated out from the centre, shaded by tall trees and as it was already hot, even at that early hour of the morning, we stood in the shade while Bernardo explained a little of the history of the city.

"Salvador de Bahia was founded in 1549 by the Portuguese who arrived by ship, fully prepared," he began. "They not only had the architectural plans for the new city, but also brought with them a civic statue, 400 settlers and 400 soldiers to defend them from the local Indian tribes." "The Portuguese were obviously very well organised," I thought. Bernardo then told us how, to start with, Salvador made its money from sugar cane, using captured Indians to work in the fields. "They were too rebellious, however," he said. "They caused so much trouble that they were replaced by slaves brought over from Africa."

With the large influx of cheap black labour, tobacco and rice were introduced to the area and cattle ranching also provided a good income. Salvador became the capital of Brazil until 1763 when this honour passed to Rio de Janeiro. "The slaves in Salvador preserved their African culture and traditions which were handed down and can still be seen in the city today," explained Bernardo. "About 80% of the current population are of African descent."

Our guide then took us across Independence Square to a bus stop where, after a short wait, we caught a local bus for a distance of about two kilometres. Around the Square, the white Regency buildings had been very grand but from there we passed through less salubrious surroundings of grimy blocks of offices and flats.

After getting off the bus, we walked for about five minutes to a large open square and stopped at a point overlooking the harbour where we were greeted by a group of gypsies. The men wore colourful shirts while the women were dressed in bright pleated skirts and white blouses with shawls tied round their heads. They were selling maps of Brazil and brightly coloured ribbons, each colour dedicated to a different African god.

James, always ready to try anything, bought a green ribbon. "This colour belongs to the god of hunting," said Bernardo. "You must make three wishes and concentrate hard on these while the ribbon is knotted round your wrist." "What happens then?" asked James. "You must keep the ribbon there and when it eventually rots away in two to three months time, your wishes will come true." James thought about his wishes while Carol tied the ribbon with a double knot around his wrist and then asked, "What happens if I take it off when I get home?" "Ah," said Bernardo, shaking his head. "You must never think of doing that! Cutting the ribbon will bring bad luck."

A few yards away was the Lacerda Elevator, a long enclosed walkway bridging the gap to a tall, slim concrete tower that rose up from the flat harbour area about 200 feet below us. "Under no circumstances must you use this Elevator," warned Bernardo. "It is notorious for muggings and murders, even during the day."

We paused for a moment to admire the view. Almost immediately below us was the Bunda Statue shaped like two teardrops supported by two inverted teardrops. The statue was surrounded by a small grassed area next to the inner harbour in which rowing boats and small yachts were moored. "Do you see that two storey white building with a central turret further back along the quayside, half hidden by palm trees? That is the Naval HQ" explained Bernardo.

Beyond this building, a long wall jutted out into the bay, providing an outer harbour in which were anchored several yachts and larger vessels, white against the deep blue of the ocean.

Across the square from where we stood on the upper level was an attractive white building, a cross between a neo-classical block of offices and St. Paul's Cathedral in London. This was the Catédral Basilica, built in the 17th century, very ornate at roof level, its white dome surmounting a huge semi-circular upper window. We crossed the square to the cathedral but when we tried to enter, we found it locked. Bernardo apologised for this. "At one time," he said, "this was the Governor's palace. Inside, it is a vision of gold, glass and wrought iron with a wonderful ceiling." We could only imagine it.

Walking through to another square, we were taken to a store selling gemstones. In the doorway, trying to entice people inside, stood a very attractive young lady of African descent in a traditional Bahian dress made of pure white cotton lace, the knee-length full skirt being in four tiers and the bodice nearly hidden by a very wide, off-the shoulder collar, again in tiers. To set off the outfit, she wore a yellow sash around her waist and a twisted turban-style white and yellow headdress, the colours showing off her dark skin to perfection. Sadly for Bernardo, we were all far more interested in the girl than the gemstones; he made no commission out of our party.

From here, we went to the old city centre where the buildings, dating back to the 17th century, were being restored. The plaster had been renovated and repainted in shades of blue, pink, lemon, green and deep gold. Between these lovely two and three storey terraced houses with their tall windows and ironwork balconies were many churches, some very baroque in design, others comparatively plain.

In Anchieta Square, we came to the church of St Francis, the large white Cross of St Francis standing proudly in front of it like a monument in the square. Although Igreja São Francisco looked plain from the outside, it is known as the "golden church" and the inside was very elaborately carved and painted in gold. It was rather overwhelming.

Attached to it was a convent and the cloisters, painted white, floored with pink marble and decorated with beautiful blue and white Portuguese tiling, looked cool and serene in contrast.

From here, we walked a short distance into the Pelhourinho district, the oldest part of the city. Near the top of a steep hill is a very wide cobbled street where two roads converge into one; this is the area where slaves were once beaten in public and sold. It was difficult now to imagine the sordid past of this street where so much suffering has taken place. The buildings have all been renovated and painted in lovely pastel shades, set off by the dark grey cobbles, and there is a wonderful view down the hill across the red-tiled roofs to the twin black and white towers of a distant church.

We were given half an hour to explore the old town by ourselves. David and I entered a shop selling traditional musical instruments and immediately became fascinated. We saw wooden pan pipes in all sizes, tied together with red and yellow string. Further along were dozens of rainmakers, made from hollowed-out lengths of bamboo, sealed at the ends, beautifully painted and filled with tiny stones or seeds that sound exactly like rain pattering on leaves when the tube is tilted. I tried out several of these and found that each instrument has its own distinctive sound. The length of pattering obtained from one tilt of the instrument also varies considerably. We found another traditional instrument, the berimbau, a long bow with a single string which is scraped or plucked and has half a coconut shell attached at the base to make the sound resonate.

Independence Square

Bahian dress

Salvador Cathedral

Anchieta Square

Pelhourinho   **Salvador from the harbour**

There were also more familiar instruments and we were encouraged to try them out in the shop. One customer was listening to the sounds produced by a selection of violins while another tested a drum set. I was very tempted to buy a rainmaker and had chosen one I liked but was reluctantly persuaded to leave it when David pointed out that at the end of the tour, we would be visiting a craft market where the instruments would probably be cheaper.

We met up with the group again to visit a section of the old city wall which had been opened as a museum. The entrance, an archway dating back to the 16th century, had obviously been used more recently as a public convenience. It smelt dreadful so David and I decided to leave the group there and we crossed the road to where several shops were selling paintings in a wide variety of styles. Particularly fascinating were scenes of the city from above; each individual building had been painted in bright colours and individuals were shown going about their business. Having seen the paintings on display in the street, we entered the shops in turn to admire the paintings inside while the other one watched for the rest of the party to emerge from the museum.

When at last they did so, Bernardo led us through a slum area of the old town where plaster was peeling from the blackened walls. The ground floors were all boarded up but washing was hung across the upper tenement windows. We hoped that the Council would find the money in due course to renovate this part of the city also, as it had a charm of its own. We then came down a steep hill to the market area near the harbour which was where our city tour finished.

David and I visited the indoor craft market which was fascinating but very expensive. T-shirts were priced from 10 reals upwards, about the same price as in England at the time but not of such good quality, and although we saw rainmakers, the wood was split and they were poorly painted and finished. The only item we would consider buying was a wooden dish shaped like a fish in rich dark jacaranda wood but the price was a steep 85 reals; we were not prepared to pay that much and the stallholders were not prepared to bargain.

We were feeling hungry by this time but even the cafés near the market were expensive. It was now mid-afternoon. We walked a little way out along the harbour wall to take some photographs; the view was lovely, the colours of the buildings on the steep hillside being reflected in the water.

We caught a bus back to Independence Square where we had a light, inexpensive snack in a restaurant before returning to our own hotel. When we made enquiries about our room at Reception, the management gave us a gift of a small silver broach in the shape of a berimbau, which we thought was a lovely gesture, and offered us a choice of three alternative rooms, all of which looked pretty neglected and run down.

We selected the one we thought was the best and then arranged for staff to repair the window which had been nailed shut, mend the shower which was running continuously and insulate some bare wires that stuck out of the wall at the back of the bed, right next to my pillow. By the time these repairs had been carried out, we just had time for a quick shower and change of clothes before leaving for an evening show in the old town.

The performance took place on the roof of one of the buildings. As we made our way along narrow cobbled pavements from where the coach dropped us off, we were hassled by young children. "Watch your belongings," warned Shelagh as a young boy laughingly pulled at her hand and others jostled around.

"Men round the outside," ordered Graham and the men in the group formed a protective circle round the women. We followed Carol into a house, climbed the stairs and on the fourth floor, found a room converted to a small bar with a door opening out on to the roof area where stone blocks had been arranged in a stepped semi-circle like a Roman amphitheatre. We bought cold drinks at the bar and sat outside on the stone blocks under the stars in the warm night air while a young, enthusiastic group put on a splendid show.

The evening began with candomblé, an African word meaning "a dance in honour of the gods." The dancers were dressed to represent various gods and the dances reflected the personalities of those gods. Red was the colour for the god of storm while red and white represented the warrior god and both these dances were full of verve and passion. Green was for the god of hunting but because he is also the god of nature, the dance was much calmer. Blue represented the goddess of the sea and also of fertility, while gold was for the god of love. The dancers were accompanied by a band using traditional instruments, mainly drums and the berimbau.

After the candomblé came capoeira, a form of dancing that originated from African martial arts. First we saw stick-dancing, a cross between a duel and Morris dancing, accompanied by the beat of drums. This was followed by a very skilled form of dancing that involves a pair of dancers kicking out at each other and spinning under each other's outstretched legs, so as to just avoid catching the other person. As the dance progressed, the tempo gradually increased, making it more and more difficult for the dancers to judge distances accurately. We were very impressed. This was followed by sequence marching to the beat of the drums and berimbau and ended with the audience joining in general dancing. It was an excellent evening.

Before the show started, David had been chatting to a Brazilian couple in the bar. They sat just in front of us and during the show, kept turning round, looking at us and smiling. The man was middle-aged and white with a slight paunch, his hair beginning to recede at the temples while the slim, dark attractive girl appeared to be in her late teens or early twenties. We thought they were probably father and daughter. As the show finished, the man asked whether we had enjoyed the performance and whether we had anything planned for the following day.

As it happened, we had a free day and had not yet decided what we were going to do. "My name is Alfonso and this is my girlfriend, Miranda" he said. "Miranda doesn't speak English but we have talked it over together and we should be honoured to show you the sights of Salvador tomorrow if you would agree to join us." After a quick glance at each other and a nod, we said we would be delighted and thanked them for their kindness. "May we drive you back to your hotel tonight?" asked Alfonso. We accepted and after letting Carol know that we would not be returning on the coach, we went with our new friends to their car which was parked just down the street.

When we reached the car, it was surrounded by a gang of small boys. They had been guarding the car and Alfonso paid them for their trouble. "It's necessary," he explained to us. "It doesn't cost a lot but if you don't pay, your car will be damaged or missing when you return." Alfonso luckily knew where our hotel was and he and Miranda drove us back and arranged to pick us up from Reception at 9am the following morning.

Day 9. Sunday 11th September.

We woke to torrential rain. Shelagh had breakfast with us and when we told her of our plans for the day, she was really worried. "You don't know these people," she said. "They may be planning to drive you somewhere quiet and rob you of all your belongings." "We've spoken to them and we trust them," we said. This did not prevent Shelagh's misgivings. "Don't take anything valuable with you," she warned. "Watch where they take you and don't get out of the car unless you think it's safe." Then, ever the concerned policewoman, she began to warn us of danger signs to watch out for until we had to start convincing ourselves that we had nothing to fear.

At 9am prompt, our new friends drew up in their car outside the hotel and came into Reception to collect us. They were both dressed very casually, Alfonso in a white T-shirt and shorts and Miranda in denim jacket and jeans with a cropped white cotton top. We waved Shelagh goodbye, told her to have a good day and not to worry and set off with our friends on a mystery tour.

Our first visit was to the Igreja of Nosso Senhor do Bonfim. As Alfonso parked the car near the church, we were surrounded by people selling bunches of different coloured ribbons like those representing the African gods. Here the custom had been adapted to Christianity and all the ribbons were printed with the words "El Senhor Do Bonfim". Drivers in Salvador hang the ribbons over the back of the interior driving mirror for protection and good fortune. Alfonso already had a bunch of ribbons fluttering from his driving mirror and he bought us a souvenir bunch of ribbons for our car back in England.

The heavy rain had by now reduced to a misty drizzle and we walked to the church without getting too wet. Built in

1745, this church is the Bahian equivalent of Lourdes. People come here from all over Bahia State and further afield to have their illnesses cured and their wishes granted.

The church was crowded but Alfonso said, "Follow me," and he and Miranda took us round to a side chapel where from every inch of ceiling hung plastic replicas of arms, legs, heads, hands, hearts and other parts of the body depending on what needed healing. The walls of the chapel were covered from floor to ceiling with literally thousands of photographs and testimonies from people who had been cured. Against one wall leant a large wooden cross, almost completely hidden by the coloured ribbons wrapped around it and messages attached to it, representing wishes of all kinds. Seeing this was quite an experience and we felt humbled by all this evidence of faith and hope.

From here, Alfonso drove us out of the city to Forte Mont Serat, one of three forts built by the Portuguese in the 16th century to defend the city. It was a low, rectangular white building standing on an elevated rain-lashed green promontory. Alfonso bought the entrance tickets, refusing to let us pay, and we went inside to find a small museum on two floors with exhibits of old pistols, revolvers and muskets in glass cases.

The two men found these fascinating but Miranda and I were less interested. While we waited for Alfonso and David, she chatted in Portuguese to some small boys visiting the fort while I took a photograph of the adjacent beach which was lovely, even in the rain; it stretched for miles round a long sandy bay fringed with houses and the occasional block of flats while a low line of hills rose up along the horizon. Beside the fort, a football pitch had been created in pink cement on the sand and floodlights had been installed on either side of the pitch so it could be used at night. Despite the weather, a game was in full swing. Brazilians seem to live for their music and football.

From here, we visited the prosperous Itapua district of Salvador where the luxury villas had verdant gardens surrounded by brick walls. The rain had by now eased to a light drizzle.

Alfonso suggested that David and I should walk down the beach to look at the Itapoan Lighthouse while he and Miranda remained behind in the car. The sandy beach was strewn with low rocks and the lighthouse with its broad horizontal red and white stripes was silhouetted against light grey skies and a slate grey sea flecked with white foam.

When we returned to the car a few moments later, we found Alfonso and Miranda making the most of our absence. We decided it was only fair to leave them alone a little longer so we went back to the beach and walked along to a picnic area, set out with concrete tables and wooden folding chairs but closed for the winter. At one end, an enormous carved wooden serpent was wrapped around the stump of a tree and further on was a stone statue of Neptune standing majestically in a chariot drawn by two sea-horses, a dolphin rearing up before them. This was probably a very popular spot in the season but by this time, the rain was falling more heavily and soaking us so we returned, interrupted the two lovebirds and continued on our way.

Our last stop before lunch was at Abaété Lagoon, surrounded by hills of very white sand. The weather was now much brighter, the rain had stopped and we all went for a walk round the lagoon and up to the top of the dunes, for a view across the dunes on the opposite side of the lagoon to the sea in the distance.

As we walked, and translating everything for the benefit of Miranda, Alfonso told us that he was 46 years old, she was 21 and he was paying for her University education. They hoped to marry when she had finished studying pharmacy in six years time. "It is usual in Brazil for a man to take a much younger wife," he said, as though we had expressed surprise at the difference in ages. "Miranda's father is twenty five years older than her mother so we do not see this as a problem."

We agreed that age was immaterial as long as they loved each other. Secretly, though, we felt that although Alfonso was clearly besotted with Miranda, her feelings for him were not so obvious. We hoped for his sake that she was not simply using him to get a degree and a well-paid job before leaving him for someone younger.

Alfonso told us that he was a civil engineering manager and owned a luxury flat with a swimming pool in Salvador plus a farm in the country covering about 2,600,000 acres. "It would take at least three days to walk round the boundary," he said proudly. "I have a manager looking after the farm while I'm away. I'm keeping a third of the land as virgin Atlantic Rainforest as I believe in conservation. The rest of the farm consists mainly of coffee, banana and rubber plantations." "Does the farm belong to your family?" we asked. "No," replied Alfonso, "land is quite cheap here and I bought it myself."

As we returned to the car park, we saw a stall with various fabrics for sale. The stall-holder was a large and very attractive Bahian African lady with a big welcoming smile. She wore a white cotton turban with a multi-coloured cotton print dress covered by a full, very fine white cotton blouse edged in lace. She was delighted when I asked if I might take a photograph.

From Abaété, we drove back along the coast towards Salvador and stopped for lunch at a churrascaria, the Rincão Gaucho Restaurant, where all the waiters were dressed as gauchos in white shirts with wide flowing sleeves and pleated baggy trousers with wide belts. The meat was speared on long swords and they used the knives from their belts to slide the meat on to customers' plates.

Luckily we arrived early while it was quiet and found a table without difficulty. Ten minutes later, people were queuing out of the door and down the street. It was clearly a very popular choice of restaurant.

Alfonso explained that what we thought was just a plastic table number was actually used as a code. "As long as the number is upright," he said, "it means that more meat is wanted and the waiters will continue to call at your table. Once everyone has sufficient, we let the waiters know by turning the number upside-down." We had a wonderful meal and, despite our protests, we were not permitted to pay anything towards it.

We insisted that we should at least buy drinks for our new friends so after the meal, they took us to a typical Brazilian Samba Bar. This was a delightful place on the roof of a building, with palm-leaf thatch high overhead and open at the sides with views across to the sea and the beaches lined with palm trees. Even when we arrived it was very busy and the tables and chairs were packed closely together. Seafood was sold with the drinks and Alfonso and Miranda opted for prawns with their beers.

David and I wanted no more to eat and settled for fresh coconut milk which was delicious and very refreshing. We stayed there chatting and eventually, at 4pm, the band arrived. The samba music was very rhythmic and catchy and all the customers stood beside their tables, jigging up and down and wriggling, writhing and shaking to the beat of the music. It was a real family affair with everyone, from elderly grandparents to babes in arms, all joining in together and having a wonderful time. It was a lovely friendly atmosphere and all too soon it was time to return to our hotel, exchange addresses with our new friends, thank them again for all their hospitality and bid them farewell.

That evening, we were going to a candomblé religious ceremony for which we had been told to wear our lightest coloured clothing, white if possible but certainly no red, purple, brown or black, including underwear, since these colours might attract evil spirits.

"They check your underwear at the entrance to the church," warned Carol. The mind boggled. "I've only got dark navy trousers," said Phil. "Will they do?" After a second's thought, Carol offered him her light blue pyjama trousers to wear for the evening. Apart from being a little on the short side, they looked fine.

We set off for the temple at 7pm and Bernardo told us that as guests, we were to remain silent throughout the ceremony and do exactly what everyone else did. "Under no circumstances refuse any food you are offered," he warned. "This would be seen as an insult."

The temple appeared to be a square bungalow painted white, set high on a hillside and reached by concrete steps over which hung a white canopy. Before we started climbing the steps, Bernardo collected us in a group on the pavement. "You will be attending a ceremony in honour of Ormolu, the Creator," he said. "Although there is one almighty deity above him who is in charge of all the gods, Ormolu ranks higher than the other deities. Animal sacrifices were carried out this morning. Only initiates are allowed to be present for that part of the proceedings."

Halfway up the steps was a small house, a temple to an intermediary between gods and men. "This intermediary behaves like a fickle child," explained Bernardo. "If you please him, you may obtain your desires but if you upset him, you may get the opposite. Since nobody is ever certain of what mood he is in, people are not really surprised if their dreams fail to come true. We haven't enough time to look at this temple so go straight up the steps to the top. When you enter the temple, do not speak and do whatever everyone else does. Remember, this is not a tourist attraction. It is an important religious ceremony and you are honoured to be allowed to attend."

At the top of the steps, ushers stood just inside the doors of the main temple directing women to the left and men to the right and we all sat on rows of wooden benches, silently taking in our surroundings.

We were at one end of a large room about thirty feet square with a tall central shrine. This was draped with and hidden by white lace curtains like a small square four-poster bed, a pot of greenery standing at the foot of each post. From the centre of the ceiling dense rows of white paper streamers radiated out to the four walls of the room; eight lights spaced evenly around the ceiling were draped in silver tinsel; and aromatic green leaves and tinsel were scattered all over the floor.

There was no glass in any of the windows, each of which had white net draped across the top and down the sides. Bernardo had explained to us earlier that this was to allow free access to the good spirits, but straw was hung across the outside of the windows to confuse and keep out the evil spirits. At the far end of the room, a small fenced-off area contained the members of the orchestra who between them had three drums, two sets of cymbals and a xylophone. The air was scented with pine and herbs.

We had arrived early for the ceremony which was due to begin at 8pm but, Brazilian time being flexible, it was an hour after that before the High Priestess, dressed in white, took her seat beside the band and the dancers appeared, also dressed entirely in white with bare feet.

The initiates, all women, wore dresses with very full, billowing long layered skirts with wide lacy shawls over their shoulders; they were accompanied by helpers, women not susceptible to possession, whose white dresses had long narrow straight skirts. The dancing then began.

As the band played a gentle rhythmic beat, the initiates slowly circled round the central shrine in an anti-clockwise direction, taking three small steps in and three small steps out, chanting and making individual graceful hand movements to call down the different gods.

While they were dancing, the congregation had to stand with their hands raised to shoulder height, palms held outwards towards the dancers, both as a sign of respect and to direct energy into the centre of the room. Every fifteen minutes or so there was a short break and the dancers, some of whom looked quite elderly, sat on the floor around the central shrine, resting, relaxing and chatting to their friends for about five minutes before continuing. We were allowed to sit while the dancers were resting but had to stand again when the dancing resumed.

After about an hour, the dancers withdrew and helpers, both male and female, emerged from a back room in a procession bearing large bowls of dry cooked rice, sago and tapioca. At the front of the procession, four men struggled to carry a stool bearing what we assumed was a statue of the god Ormolu, completely hidden in swathes of white lace; whatever it was, it was obviously very heavy. This was set on a shrine behind the High Priestess and a male helper came round the congregation and "beat" everyone by touching them on either shoulder with a stick.

The helpers then gave each of us a tablespoonful of rice in our right hands to eat with our left hands, and this was followed by the sago and tapioca. There was also a bowl with stringy yellow bits in it like melted cheese. I ate very slowly so I could only hold the rice and sago in my hand but food was served until all the bowls were empty. We were then allowed to sit down.

We were later told that ceremonies to honour one or more of the gods are held every day of the week so this is perhaps a way of feeding the poorest people of the city while encouraging them to join the religious cult.

The dancers soon returned and we again stood to redirect the energy towards them with the palms of our hands. The circling and chanting then continued until, one by one, the dancers began shaking and convulsing, their eyes closing or turning unseeingly upwards. The helpers rushed to support them and to untie the shawls of the initiates before retying them, knotted at the back instead of at the front. These dancers were then led into the back room where, we were told later, the helpers identify which of the gods has possessed each of them. They then dress each initiate in the costume and colours of the relevant god.

We were quite shocked when a woman in the congregation, two rows behind our group, also began violently shaking and convulsing in her seat. We had to move the benches and assist her to the centre of the room from where the helpers led her to the back room with the initiates.

At this point, Carol signalled to us that it was time to leave and we all quietly filed out of the door. When we were outside, she told us that the ceremony would continue until dawn the next day. It was now 11pm and we had to be up at 4am the following morning to continue our journey.

On the way back to the hotel, Bernardo told us, "The first time someone goes into a trance, the helpers carry out an initiation ceremony. They use a sacred knife to make a cut in the shape of a cross on the chest, forehead and back of the person who has been possessed, the person being completely unaware of this until they come out of the trance. That person is then an initiate and is expected to take part in future ceremonies."

He added, "A trance can last any length of time, even up to two weeks. It is a big decision to make if you have a job as you know you will be dismissed for absenteeism. It is impossible for anyone to practise their religion as an initiate and to hold down a job at the same time."

We asked whether it had been known for anyone from a tour group to go into a trance. We were told that it had never happened so far and we thought it unlikely as we were all rather sceptical. Nonetheless, having seen someone from the congregation succumb, it was still a slightly worrying thought.

4

MANAUS

Day 10. Monday 12th September.

By 5am, we were on our way to the airport and were rewarded for our early start with a glorious golden sunrise over the sea. Later, on the flight to Manaus, we were able to look down upon the River Amazon, reflecting the light as it meandered through the jungle. "Look," said Nigel from the seat in front of us. "Oxbow lakes," and there below us was a series of golden curves against the dark background of trees. "That reminds me of geography lessons from many years ago," I said to David.

According to the itinerary, we were supposed to stop on the way to Manaus for a tour of Brasilia, the capital of Brazil since 1960. We had seen photographs of Brasilia's wide open spaces and futuristic architecture and were looking forward to seeing the buildings themselves. Unfortunately, the flight was delayed and Carol came round to tell us that the tour had been cancelled and that we would have to remain on board the aircraft at Brasilia. We were really disappointed and James and Graham made this very clear to Carol, although there was nothing she could do about it.

The delays also meant that we did not arrive in Manaus until mid-afternoon, leaving little time for sightseeing. In the coach from the airport to the hotel, Carol informed us that Manaus is the capital of Amazonas. "It is situated on the Rio Negro only six miles from its confluence with the Rio Solimões, the two rivers converging to form the River Amazon," she said. "This point is famous. It is known as the "Meeting of the Waters" because the black waters of the Rio Negro and the "white" clay-coloured waters of the Rio Solimões flow side by side for several miles without mixing. You may be able to spot it from the plane when we leave Manaus tomorrow morning."

"Until recently," she went on, "the city was only accessible by air or river. Despite this, Manaus grew rapidly during the rubber boom of the late 19th century. Under Eduardo Ribeira, the State Governor at that time, it became a gracious city of palaces, mansions and luxury homes built on wide shady boulevards with statues and with fountains playing in the squares. It was the first Brazilian city to have trolley buses and the second, after Rio, to have electric street lighting."

"With the collapse of the rubber market at the start of the first World War," she continued, "the city went into temporary decline, but in 1966 Manaus was designated a "Free Trade Zone" and began to prosper again. Manaus now has more than two million inhabitants and specialises in the manufacture of electronics. Goods can be imported here, tax free, from all over the world and because prices are much cheaper here than elsewhere in Brazil, people come from all over the country to purchase goods. The port and airport are always busy."

As we drove through the city, our initial impression was that although the streets were still wide, the palaces and luxury mansions of Manaus had all been replaced by high-rise blocks of flats and offices. The city's economy may have been thriving but away from the centre, poverty, neglect and decay seemed all too apparent.

Outside, our hotel blended in with its surroundings, part of a dirty tenement building block several stories high, with litter strewn across the pavements. Inside, however, the Reception area was surprisingly opulent with wooden parquet flooring and gleaming tiled walls.

When we went up to our room, we found it spacious and comfortable. The spotlessly clean en-suite bathroom was reached by three tiled steps, with its walls beautifully tiled from floor to ceiling and a shining tiled floor, a real contrast to our room in Salvador. We had no time to admire it now, however. Pausing only long enough to lock our luggage in the room, we set off with the group only minutes later on a walk to the city centre.

We stopped in a large square below the famous Opera House. The square was edged with trees and tiled with black and white Portuguese mosaic swirls, supposedly representing the Meeting of the Waters. In the centre of the square was a memorial statue.

"Eduardo Ribeira originally arranged for the Opera House to be built," said Carol. "He imported all the materials and artists from Europe and it was once considered one of the four best theatres in the world." We gazed in awe at the Opera House, constructed in classical style with tall slender white marble columns supporting the entrance to the building, pink exterior walls with contrasting white reliefs and a glittering golden dome decorated with tiles in slate blue and red.

From the square, we climbed one of the flights of pink steps with white balustrades to reach the entrance to the Opera House. We felt that somehow this splendour was rather incongruous in a city which, despite its wide paved streets, still seemed to have the atmosphere of a frontier town.

Inside, the theatre was just as beautiful, in pink stone and white marble with "Old Master" paintings on walls and ceilings. We were not allowed to enter the auditorium because a charity show for the disabled was taking place but Steve had a video camera and peeped round the door. He let me have a quick look through the viewfinder and the scene was magically lit by the camera, showing a large auditorium with chandeliers and a stage which appeared larger than those of most London theatres.

"Outside," Carol told us, "the builders incorporated rubber into the black driveway in front of the Opera House to muffle the sound of carriage wheels and horses hooves, so as not to disturb any performance going on inside."

While we were in the theatre, the skies turned black, the angry clouds lit with flashes of jagged forked lightning as Manaus was hit by a tropical storm. As rain fell in torrents and thunder rumbled loudly around the city, we sat it out in the theatre's small refreshment area, drinking bottled water and cola. The storm vanished as quickly as it had come and as soon as the rain had ceased, Carol hurried us across the town to the harbour area. On the way, we passed the Cathedral and an impressive bus station, half hidden behind rows of domed perspex bus shelters where crowds of people were queuing to return home at the end of a day's work.

We found the harbour tightly packed with white-painted double-decker ships anchored side by side. Many of these were preparing to sail shortly to other ports on the Amazon and were a frenzy of shouting and activity, their open lower decks heavily festooned with hammocks, each new passenger jostling for hanging space between his neighbours.

Manaus Opera House

Manaus city centre

Manaus harbour

Tabatinga airport

Moneychangers in Leticia

Some of the ships had blue tarpaulins draped round the decks, whether to give privacy or to keep out the weather we were not quite sure.

On the quay, young men were holding out metal bowls containing something that looked exactly like large potato crisps; these seemed to be a favourite snack for a river trip as many of the passengers were buying them. "What do you think those are?" asked David. "I don't know," I said. "Let's try some." We bought a handful and found them crisp and salty and tasting remarkably like potato crisps but a little more chewy. We found Carol who told us they were dried plantain, a plant from the banana family.

By this time, it was getting dark so we made our way back to the hotel where there was a rooftop restaurant, open to the stars and overlooking the city lights. We had a delicious meal of tender, succulent steak and retired to bed at 9pm, absolutely exhausted after our early morning start.

5

LETICIA

Day 11. Tuesday 13th September.

David and I woke at 5am to the sound of rain lashing against the window. Listening to it I said, "I know we agreed last night to get up early to see some more of the city before breakfast, but now I'm not so sure."

David walked over to the window and peered round the curtain. At that moment there was a double flash of lightning followed almost immediately by a loud rumble of thunder and the rain threw itself against the window pane in a renewed frenzy. "It may have blown over by the time we're ready," he said, "but I must admit it doesn't look very inviting at the moment." "Let's forget it," I suggested. "Good idea," and David made his way back into our warm comfortable bed, snuggled down and went back to sleep.

By 8am, after the usual lavish Brazilian breakfast, we were on our way to the airport. Our flight took us over the Amazon but from the aircraft we were unable to identify the "Meeting of the Waters". We flew quite low over the jungle and could even make out the different coloured foliage of the individual trees.

A couple of hours later, we landed at Tabatinga in Brazil. "This is the prettiest airport I've ever seen," I told David, as the aeroplane taxied to a halt beside lush green lawns, palm trees and beds of roses, gleditsia and flowering shrubs with leaves of red, green and gold. Leaving the aircraft, we wandered down a slabbed path between the flower beds to the small arrivals building. This was a single room divided down the middle by a partition, the passengers crammed into one half and the staff in the other half.

From here, we watched through the glass of the entrance door as two men manhandled the luggage out of the hold a few cases at a time, loaded them on to a hand trolley, dragged the trolley to the airport building, unloaded the cases into the staff's half of the building and went back for more. The luggage was then filtered out to us, one case at a time. This procedure seemed to take a very long time but after about an hour, we all had our luggage and boarded a very ancient bus that trundled us about a mile down the road from Portuguese-speaking Tabatinga in Brazil across the border to Spanish-speaking Leticia in Colombia.

On the way, Carol told us that although Colombia is a poor country, the people of Leticia have benefited from their proximity to Tabatinga and Brazil. "Because Bogota is over 2,000 kilometres away, Spanish-speaking television programmes were not broadcast as far as Leticia," she explained. "Then the Colombian Government discovered, much to their horror, that the children in this area had been watching Brazilian television programmes in their friends' homes in Tabatinga and spoke Portuguese more fluently than Spanish. As a result, a satellite dish was installed in Leticia in 1991 so that people could receive Spanish-speaking programmes."

"Only five years ago," she added, "there was no electricity in Leticia until the inhabitants bought it from Brazil across the border. Again there was an outcry and as a result, the Colombian Government provided a powerful generator and now the village sells electricity to Brazil."

The ancient bus took us to our hotel, the Anaconda, situated on the main street. This was simple, clean and pleasant. It had a lovely swimming pool with tables and chairs at one end of the patio. On the opposite side were some palm trees in which were perched two beautiful blue and yellow macaws.

After a light lunch beside the pool, we had a couple of hours to explore the town and to change our Brazilian money before our excursion bus left at 3pm. "You won't need any Colombian currency," Carol told us. "Brazilian reals and U.S. dollars are both acceptable here. However, don't keep too many reals. Remember you will be leaving Colombia tomorrow on an Amazon cruise which finishes in Peru. U.S. dollars will be the standard currency while you're on board the cruise ship."

David and I had some U.S. dollars and since we no longer needed our remaining Brazilian reals, we decided to change these for Peruvian sols. We found a whole street of money changers, each in his own individual little wooden chalet, the chalets lined up in a row under the trees down the centre of the road. Starting at the top of the street, we stopped at each chalet to ask the rate of commission and how many sols we would get to the real. We soon found that the further we went from the main road, the better the exchange rate.

Down the hill towards the river, the concrete shops, houses and hotels gave way to wooden houses on stilts with palm thatch roofs but having spent time changing our money, we had to forget about exploration and return to the hotel for the afternoon excursion.

The bus waiting outside our hotel was even more ancient and dilapidated than the one which had brought us from the airport. There were hints of previous luxury in the remains of red padded leather round the windows but now the steps were rusted right through in places. There were holes in the floor of the central gangway so we held on to the seat backs as we walked down the bus, just in case we fell through. Springs stuck up through the seats and the glass in several windows had been replaced with cellophane.

We had only travelled a hundred yards down the road when the engine died and the driver had great difficulty in starting up again. He managed it at last, just as we anticipated having to get out and push. He also had problems when he wanted to turn a corner, having to drag the steering wheel round to full lock and take the corner very wide at about 3mph, the bus screeching and protesting as we gradually inched round.

Luckily the harbour was not far away. Alighting from the bus, we walked across a flat concreted area and climbed down the metal ladder at the far end on to the grassy bank. From here we made our way down a long, steep gangplank with only a swinging rope handhold to help us to keep our balance until we came to the river mud; this we crossed on planks and straw, with a final plank on to a large square pontoon floating in the river, on the far side of which two motor boats were moored, waiting for us.

Once settled in the boats, we sped down the Amazon for about two kilometres to the Yahurcacas Lakes, famous for their giant Victoria Regia water lilies. On the way, we were lucky enough to see a school of pink river dolphins in the distance, cavorting in the water and occasionally leaping into the air.

We realised that we had arrived when we spotted, on ten foot high stilts on top of the bank, a large sign bearing a painting of the water lilies. We clambered out of the boats on to the flat mud which was luckily fairly firm, walked across to the river bank towering above us and climbed a ladder to the top. Our guide told us that the Amazon falls to its lowest level in October but between January and May, rises about 40 feet at this point, sometimes higher. For this reason, even the houses on top of the banks are built on stilts.

The lakes were about five minutes walk inland from the river. When we arrived, our guide pointed out the high water mark on trees around the lake, about 10 feet above our heads. "Despite the difficulties, people live in the flood area because the river refertilises the land each year," he said. "There is always good soil for cultivation."

There were two lakes, the largest crossed by a wooden bridge. The lakes were entirely covered with huge water lily leaves and we wandered round to admire them from various angles. "These giant water lilies only grow in still water," said our guide. "They obviously manage to survive the river currents during the annual flood periods," I thought. "They must be completely submerged at certain times of the year."

Although the double flowers, white tinged with pink, were not particularly large, the leaves were enormous, each about four foot in diameter and pancake flat but turned up all around the edges, showing their red undersides. We were told that each leaf was able to support the weight of a child but we decided not to test their strength as we were also told that the lakes were full of piranha and possibly anaconda.

Climbing up the river bank

Victoria Regia water lily leaves, Yahurcacas Lakes

Walkway to Tabatinga Market

River boats at Tabatinga

As we made our way back down the mud bank to the motor boats, we noticed a black shape in the river, swimming towards us. This turned out to be a very tame capybara and was probably a pet as it came rushing out of the water to greet us. It took a fancy to Jack, ran up to him, sniffed him and grabbed him round the leg with its front paws. Jack had great difficulty in shaking it off and ran for the motor boat with the capybara lolloping along behind while we all stood watching, unsympathetically doubled up with laughter.

On the way back upriver, we saw the dolphins again. "They are sacred to the Indians," explained our guide. "Some tribes believe that at night, the dolphins change into handsome young men, irresistible to women. Many an otherwise unexplained pregnancy has been blamed on the dolphins."

On the way back, we called at Tabatinga market. Trying to find space to berth the boats was like trying to find a car parking space in an English town on market day. We had to queue until someone else left and then slide quickly into the vacant spot. Once the boats were moored, we crossed the mud and climbed the ladders. The market was reached by a high, rickety walkway above a ripe-smelling open sewer.

At the back of the market, wooden walkways passed the entrances to houses built on stilts above the river mud. As we walked round, we were able to see inside some of these stilt houses. They each had two rooms, the one nearest the walkway containing a table and chairs, the one at the rear containing the cooking stove and hammocks.

Back at the hotel that night, David made the mistake of finishing his meal with peaches and cream which gave him food poisoning. He was up half the night with diarrhoea.

Day 12. Wednesday 14th September.

Our first Colombian breakfast was a disappointment after the luscious feasts of Brazil - nothing but a thin slice of starfruit, bread, butter, jam and coffee. Our cases had to be packed and in the lobby by 10am and while we waited for them to be collected for loading on to the cruise ship, most of us had our shoes cleaned by the local shoeshine boy who was touting for business in the lobby.

He was a cheerful young lad with an enormous grin so we were happy to give him some work. "Right," Karl said to him when he had finished the last pair, "it's your turn now," He persuaded the lad to sit in a chair, crouched on the floor in front of him and proceeded to clean his shoes. The boy looked bewildered at first; it was probably the first time this had ever happened to him. His face then took on an expression of pure delight and at the end, he cheekily told Karl to give his shoes an extra polish with the cloth.

Once the cases had been collected, we were free for the rest of the morning but David still felt unwell and had to rush back to the hotel from time to time so we could only venture a short distance. We admired a beautiful flame tree covered in brilliant scarlet blossoms and some flowering shrubs in the village centre and looked at the nearby shops. In one of the souvenir shops, I was tempted by a lovely brown calabash painted with the outline of a curled-up cat and I also liked a fish made of a multi-coloured Colombian stone; however, although I considered buying both of these, David was not too keen on them so I saved my money.

Back by the pool, David started feeling dizzy with dehydration and sat with his head between his knees. On Carol's advice, he struggled to drink two half-litre bottles of cola to replace the lost liquids and salts but this seemed to make very little difference. We were supposed to leave at noon to walk the mile or so to the harbour but David was convinced he would be unable to make it so Carol ordered a taxi.

When the taxi arrived, I went with David so that if he felt dizzy again, I could help him to climb down the ladders and ramps, cross the mud and negotiate the floating pontoon. As we were driven slowly down the road to the harbour, we passed the rest of our party who had already set off on foot and they all waved and gave the "thumbs up" sign.

6

AMAZON CRUISE

At the pontoon, where two motor boats were waiting to transport us to our cruise ship, we met a group of Americans who would be joining us on the next stage of our journey. David explained his predicament and we were allowed to go to the front of the queue to travel on the first boat across. Once David was safely on board the Rio Amazonas, our home for the next three nights, I was able to photograph the rest of our party arriving.

Before setting sail, we had to fill in immigration forms to leave Colombia and enter Peru. We handed these to the Captain with our passports so that he could pass them to Customs when they boarded our ship a short way upriver. We then made our way to the dining room for lunch, the anchor was raised and our cruise began.

After the meal, we were told where to find the lifejackets and were allocated our rooms, all of which were on the upper deck. After sorting out our luggage which had been piled in a heap on the front deck, we then had the problem of carrying it up the steep narrow central metal stairway to the cabins. It was quite a struggle trying to hold on to the handrail with one hand to balance while carrying a heavy case up in front with the other. The alternative was to drag the case up from below and behind.

Our cabin was small but comfortable with a window, twin beds, a tiny wardrobe, washbasin, shower and toilet. All the water came straight from the River Amazon but filtered drinking water was always available in the dining room at all times so we had to remember to take some of this filtered water to our cabin at night for cleaning our teeth.

That afternoon, we were introduced to Captain Sanchez and his crew and we explored our ship, the Rio Amazonas, probably about a quarter the size of a cross-Channel ferry, before relaxing and watching the passing scenery.

"We shall be travelling upstream", Captain Sanchez informed us. "Although you may think the Amazon river looks quite wide at this point, it is almost impossible to get a clear view from bank to bank. Because there are so many islands, you will never be able to appreciate the river's full width. In places, it is four miles across and it is full of submerged sandbanks which change their position with the river currents. For this reason, we always travel with our sister ship, the El Arca."

"On our last journey downstream," put in one of the crew, "we went aground on a sandbank three times and El Arca went aground twice. On each occasion, all the passengers had to be transferred to the sister ship until tugs had pulled the trapped vessel free." We fervently hoped that this would not happen on our trip, particularly as two of the transfers had apparently taken place in the middle of the night.

The Captain advised us that the Amazon is noted for its sunsets which take place at around 6pm every evening, so at the appointed time, we all made sure we were out on the top deck. We were not disappointed. The sky was mainly clear but there were a few clouds along the horizon to emphasise the deepening golden hues which were also reflected in the calm waters of the river. We stayed there, drinking in the glorious colours until the blue overhead had deepened to navy and the last of the gold had faded from view.

Even after dark it was very pleasant on deck, warm but with a gentle breeze which kept the mosquitoes away. We found it delightful and very relaxing to watch the turbulent water at the stern of the ship, white in the moonlight. The stars seemed very clear and bright in a velvety black sky, undimmed by city lights.

After the meal, we spent most of the evening on deck, chatting and getting to know some of our fellow travellers from the States. Although David was still not eating anything, he was already feeling much better and his system was beginning to settle down.

Day 13. Thursday 15th September.

We were awake early and up at 5am to go on a jungle walk. It was just getting light, the river grey in the early morning mist. From our cabin window, we could see that we were moored by the river bank and El Arca was moored nearby. When we were ready, we made our way to the dining room where we were offered a biscuit and a cup of hot coffee to bring us round and sustain us on our walk. There were two guides on board and at 6am, the Americans went ashore with Moazir while we went with Dino, taking a different route.

Despite the early hour, some of the local children had come down to the river to see the cruise ships and watch the visitors come ashore. The children were dressed in grubby T-shirts and shorts and had bare feet but they all looked well fed and happy.

Near the start of our walk, we passed several wooden huts built on stilts, with steps up to the entrance door and palm leaf roofing. One family came to the doorway of their hut to greet us with welcoming smiles as we went by. Dino led us along a well-walked trail to a clearing where he paused and climbed on to a fallen tree over four feet in circumference and at least forty feet in length.

"The trees in the Amazon jungle have a very shallow rooting system as there is no goodness in the soil below the top six inches," he explained. "This means that they have very little stability and blow over very easily." He then added, "You are now in secondary jungle that has been subjected to slash and burn techniques followed by the cultivation of crops. After two or three years, when the land is no longer fertile, the villagers abandon it for the jungle to take over again while they clear a new area."

He told us that the growth we could see had been regenerated over about six years. Although the trees were well spaced and plenty of light filtered down to the forest floor, many of the trees were already more than thirty feet tall with trunks three to four feet in circumference with saplings growing in between and plenty of green undergrowth that to us looked quite impressive; however, Dino told us that full recovery would take about sixty years.

As we continued on our way, Dino pointed out various plants that have been used for medicinal purposes by the Indians for many centuries and are now being exploited by the developed world. He was just telling us about one plant whose root had a similar use to aspirin when he was suddenly interrupted by a loud yelp from Jack, who had brushed a liana aside with his hand and had been stung by a caterpillar about three inches in length with long bright orange hairs sticking out all over its body.

Dino assured him that although the sting was painful, it would only hurt for a short time. "Please don't rest your hands on any tree trunks or branches" he added, pointing out lines of small red ants running up and down. "These can deliver a painful bite".

On the ground we saw some huge ants, over an inch in length, which we carefully avoided. Dino pointed out round, black termite nests the size of footballs, high up on the lianas which are eventually pulled down by the weight. James, just in front of me, gently tugged at one of the lianas and it felt as though half the forest had come down on my head. I spent the next ten minutes brushing ants out of my hair and off my back and telling James exactly what I thought of his actions. He just laughed!

Dino then showed us the entrance to a tarantula hole, about three inches in diameter, and told us that as tarantulas are nocturnal creatures, the hole was probably occupied. We decided not to check whether the owner was at home. "The Indians tease the spider out, capture it and cook it as a delicacy," Dino told us.

Further on we came to a tree related to the rubber tree. Dino made a small shallow cut in the bark with his knife and a white milky liquid flowed out. "Taste that and tell me what you think," he said. We each put a finger to the liquid and touched it to our tongues. It had a pleasant sweetish taste, a little like milk of magnesia. "That's right," said Dino, "it is used as a cure for indigestion, the same as milk of magnesia is used in your country. Being sticky, it is also collected by village teachers to use as a paste in school."

"Rubber is also grown in this area," Dino added, describing how some of the liquid sap is spread in a thin film across the ground, where it dries in minutes.

"Some of this thin rubber sheet is used by the Indians to make shoes or bags, but the majority is put into large airtight containers where it stays soft. It is then sent away to be vulcanised for rubber tyres".

About an hour after we had set off, we returned to our cruise ship and found the local children still waiting on the shore. Karl had come on holiday well prepared; he had a bag full of balloons some of which he handed out, much to the delight of the children. Our last view of them as we drew away from the bank was of small faces half hidden by different coloured balloons in various stages of inflation.

Back on board, we were ready for breakfast, a simple meal of bread, butter and jam, tea or coffee. At this stage, David was still not prepared to risk eating anything and was not feeling particularly hungry in any case. After the rest of us had finished our meal, Dino told us a little about our next port of call, the village of San Pablo, where there is a leper hospital founded by missionaries.

"Until comparatively recently," he said, "the natives gave the people from San Pablo a wide berth and refused to trade with them because they thought leprosy was highly contagious. When they eventually realised that, even after many years, the missionaries remained healthy, they gradually lost their fear and a community has grown up around the hospital. You will see the children selling wooden carvings made by the lepers."

We spent the next couple of hours watching the river banks slip past. We saw occasional native huts and people beside the river, some of them fishing. However, probably because my eyes were not properly attuned to the surroundings, I could see no signs of wildlife at all, not even a bird. There also seemed to be no sounds other than that of the ship's engine, the rushing water and our own voices.

Eventually we arrived at San Pablo. David decided to stay on board as he had no energy but the rest of us went ashore. Children came running down the banks to greet us and each of us soon found that we had a child on either side, slipping a hand into ours and leading us up the banks and into the village. A thunderstorm broke and I gently detached my hands to put on a waterproof. As soon as I had done so, my hands were grabbed again. The children seemed oblivious to the rain.

"Como se llama?" asked one of my little guides tentatively. My Spanish was no better than my Portuguese but I guessed that she was asking my name. "Valerie," I replied. I was met with blank looks. Either I had misinterpreted the question or the name was too outlandish for them. "Val-er-ie," I tried again, more slowly. Then, trying to simplify things, "Val". Still the blank looks so I tried throwing the question back to them. This was far more successful. "Maria," smiled one; "Anna," beamed the other. So at least I had correctly interpreted what they were asking.

By now, the rain had stopped and we had reached the village which was surprisingly neat. A concrete pathway shining with pools of water led between the wooden huts with their corrugated iron roofs and neatly cut lawns and shrubs. Many of the huts had their own little gardens where they grew fruit, vegetables and rose bushes. There were also a few electricity cables and street lights. It looked quite suburban. Anna pulled at my hand and pointed to one of the huts where a ginger domestic cat sat on the sill of an open window. "Mia casa," she said proudly. We continued walking uphill on concrete paths and steps until we came to the hospital, situated above the village.

Our cruise ship

Children with balloons

Amazonian village

Boy with pet monkey   View from artist's studio

The children were not allowed into the hospital area and waited outside for us to return. We entered through a long wooden common room with benches on either side and plenty of openings to allow the air to circulate and catch any slight breeze. Here several patients sat in the shade in silence and rested. This room led to a large open courtyard with four wards around it, one for the women, the others for the men.

Dino had come with us and explained that leprosy starts with a loss of feeling in the hands; then the bones gradually shrink and become deformed. "Although the damage cannot be reversed, it can be arrested," he said. "There are currently thirty men and six women being treated here."

One woman in the central courtyard had only quarter inch stumps for fingers and thumbs but had somehow managed to hold a needle and create beautiful embroidered cloths which she was selling.

A male patient bravely sang a solo for us in a weak quavering voice. We all applauded him and I put some money into a box for donations. I resisted buying any embroidery or carvings which I did not want but I felt really guilty about this.

Most people bought white wood carvings of birds and animals on impulse but those who bought the larger, more impressive-looking carvings regretted it later as they were quite heavy and added considerably to the weight and bulk of their luggage.

As soon as we left the hospital the children grabbed our hands again and my youngest girl, Maria, presented me with a pink hibiscus flower. They were most attractive children with dark shining hair and eyes and honey-brown skin, dressed in T-shirts and short cotton skirts or shorts. Most were barefoot but some wore sandals. They led us back to the river bank where everyone tried to sell us more carvings, even after we were back on board ship. The children then waited on the mud banks until the ship departed and we waved them goodbye.

Once they were out of sight, we went into the dining room for a typical shipboard lunch of manioc strips in mayonnaise, rice, plantains, fish and bread and butter, followed by triangles of pastry with a thin custard layer. We found it rather tasteless and stodgy but it was nutritious and filling and would no doubt have been considered a banquet by the villagers .

That afternoon Ed, one of the Americans, put on a one-man show for the passengers and crew. He was a professional magician, very good at sleight of hand and told us that, back home in Arkansas, people travelled within a 500 mile radius to come and watch his act. Considering he had very few props with him, it was excellent entertainment.

That evening as the sun set, we all put on lifejackets and set off in the ship's little motor boats to hear the sounds of the jungle at night. We had put on plenty of insect repellent as the boats would be motionless in the water for a time.

Dino warned us that fish are more active at night and told us not to be surprised if one jumped into the boat. We were rather sceptical about this. As we motored towards the shore in the gathering dusk, bats flew overhead from the treetops. We were asked to keep silent, the engines were cut and we drifted along with the current, listening to cicadas and frogs and the whine of an occasional mosquito. I felt a little disappointed as I had hoped to hear the distant roaring of howler monkeys.

Dino kept shining his torch into the reeds to spot the eyes of alligators glowing red in the light. When he saw some, he paddled in close, leant over the edge of the boat and tried to catch the reptiles. At the third attempt, he caught a four foot long white bellied caiman that he held firmly and showed to us. The caiman remained motionless while we all felt its skin which was dry and smooth and not at all scaly. Dino then released it into the water.

In the meantime, rather worryingly, our cruise ship had continued to sail upriver with all lights blazing and had vanished from view. There was also no sign of the other motor boat and I wondered what would happen if our engine failed, then hurriedly put the thought out of my mind. Luckily the engine started again all right and we sped upriver after the ship.

Suddenly Jack let out a startled yell and something white hurtled across the boat just missing David's shoulder before splashing into the river. "I warned you about the fish," said Dino, laughing at Jack's shocked expression. A fish had leapt out of the water, hit Jack on the side of his face and somehow still had enough momentum to carry it across the boat and back into the water. It was so unexpected that it took us all by surprise; the silence was broken and we all started laughing and chatting. After his experiences with the capybara, the caterpillar and now the fish, we decided Jack must have some sort of affinity with other living creatures.

We continued our journey upriver and not long afterwards, we caught sight of our ship's lights in the distance and we were soon climbing back on board.

Day 14. Friday 16th September.

At dinner on the previous evening, we had been asked to collect together anything that we could use for bartering, from old clothes to make-up and first aid items. Bartering would play an important part in our visit this morning to the Bora Indians. David and I needed most of our luggage for the rest of the holiday but decided we could manage without our first aid kit and sewing kit as our leader could probably provide any such necessities. We also had a few sweets with us.

Shortly after breakfast, we disembarked at the village of Santa Lucia. We made our way up the gently sloping banks where there were two wooden handrails with branches laid across the ground between them.

As before, the children were waiting for us, grabbed us by the hands and led us quickly up the hill and into the main community hut, a large circular building of wooden uprights, each spaced about an inch apart and held in place by curved horizontal poles tied at the top and bottom of each post. Wooden roof beams ran from the outer wall to a central apex, the roof being covered in leaf thatch. Souvenirs hung from the walls and roof and bench seats ran all round the inside of the perimeter wall. The children remained outside the hut as we entered.

We were invited to seat ourselves on the benches and while Dino spoke to the chief, the tribal dancers stood waiting. The women wore red knee-length straight cotton skirts and grass tops which hung almost down to waist level. They also wore short grass fringes around their lower arms and their calves and green and white woven palm leaf headdresses. The men were dressed in grass skirts and grass tops and wore similar short grass fringes on their upper arms and lower legs and palm-leaf circlets on their heads.

After the chief had welcomed us to the village in a little speech which was translated by Dino, the show began. We had been promised an anaconda dance and a spider monkey dance so we were expecting something spectacular but the first dance was a shambles and apparently completely unrehearsed. It consisted of all the dancers holding hands in a circle; the chief then sang and pulled the circle to left or right while the others followed as best they could. At the end, the chief cheered so we, and the dancers, knew when the dance was over.

Early on, David had made the mistake of pushing a couple of fruit drops between the wooden posts that made up the wall to the children waiting outside and all through the performance, we had little fingers poking us in the back through the wall and loud whispers of "Miss, Miss!"

The second dance was much better as everyone followed a musician with a drum and pipe and took three steps forward and two back, in a line around the hut. Again the chief cheered to indicate when the dance had come to an end. After we had all applauded, we were invited to join the dancers in a repeat of this second dance and at the end, we were each given a present. I received a palm leaf headdress while David was given a hairy nut. Then it was time for the bargaining to begin.

We soon found that the Bora were not interested in practical items like our mending kit or first aid plasters. Sweets were more popular and we found that the going rate for a bracelet made of nuts and berries was one fruit drop while two fruit drops purchased a necklace. A lipstick bought us a musical instrument, consisting of a gourd with seeds inside it, held on a stick, while David was given a genuine native bow and two arrows in exchange for one dollar and a sunhat.

It was all good fun but I had very mixed feelings about the way in which we, and other tourists, were contributing to the natives becoming dissatisfied with their simple way of life. Most of the women wore make-up and the few not dancing wore Western clothes and, although it seemed wrong to begrudge them what we take for granted and they obviously wanted, I felt that these things were not actually bringing them happiness.

Carol called our group together and leaving the Americans here to continue bartering, we went by motor boat up one of the tributaries of the Amazon to visit a Peruvian artist in his studio home. We were told that he was world-famous and had shown his work in art exhibitions around the world (although not in the United Kingdom) and that there had recently been an article about his paintings in Time Life magazine.

As our boat pulled in to shore, the usual cluster of children was waiting to grab us by the hands and lead us up through the village. This village was also very neat and tidy with concrete pathways between the houses but was more picturesque than San Pablo because the roofs of the houses were thatched rather than made of corrugated iron. This was clearly another privileged community as electricity cables hung from telegraph poles along the main street and there was an occasional street lamp.

One of my two little girls shyly asked, "Su nombre?" This time, I knew that she was asking my name so I thought I would simplify matters and answered "Anna." This met with instant approval and my companions informed me that they were called Gleditsia and Lella.

The studio was located at the top of the hill and had a large balcony with views across the village to the river. While the children waited outside, the artist invited us in. "Please help yourselves to food and wine," he said, indicating a side table laden with glasses of red and white wine and bowls of bananas.

We felt unable to walk round and look at the paintings while we were each clutching a banana in one hand and a glass of wine in the other so we wandered out on to the balcony where two small blue parrots with bright orange-yellow breasts were feeding from a bowl of dried fruit and seeds. The view was stunning and we could see where the tributary joined the Amazon about a mile away.

Our host was a larger than life figure, tall and well built with dark smiling eyes in a brown tanned face, dark curly hair, moustache and bearded chin. He wore a red cotton headband across his forehead and a loose white cotton shirt with enormous pockets at hip level, hanging outside his dark trousers. He gave a strong impression of enjoying life to the full and clearly loved painting. Once we had disposed of our glasses and banana skins, he put on a record of the Amazonian Symphony in order to create the right ambience while we wandered around and looked at his work displayed on the studio walls.

The styles varied enormously and while most of the paintings were semi-abstract with a lot of swirl and movement and a vivid mix of colours, there were also portraits in sepia on a white background. We were then taken downstairs below the studio to see where the bark canvases are framed and boxed up for export.

James asked for an autograph. There seemed to be no paper available so the artist signed the back of James' white T-shirt with a flamboyant signature in black ink. Steve, who was wearing a black T-shirt, then asked if he might have a autograph as well. The artist painted it on in white and then stood back and flicked orange spatters of paint around the signature. It looked very effective.

As we came out of the studio, we found the children standing in groups waiting for us. One or two of the older children were carrying younger siblings and a couple of the boys were playing with pet monkeys. Some of the children grabbed our hands again to take us back to the boat. Lella changed her loyalties and went to Mary but another little girl immediately took her place. This child was losing her skirt which was coming adrift from its elastic waistband. As it happened, I had a safety pin on me so I pinned the skirt back together and she was really pleased.

We returned to our cruise ship for lunch. After the meal, the ship pulled in to the shore and we were offered the option of a boat trip up one of the narrower tributaries. The early afternoon temperature was up in the 100°s Fahrenheit, we were told there would be no shelter and we were already slightly sunburnt from the morning's excursion, so David and I decided to stay on board in the shade.

We watched as those taking the excursion climbed into the motor boat which then waited at the landing stage in the scorching heat for at least ten minutes before the local guide came on board and it finally sped upstream. We were really thankful we had decided to stay on the ship.

Our friend Shelagh went on the excursion and told us later that the boat had entered a very shallow tributary, not much wider than the boat. "We kept going aground," she said excitedly, "and each time, the guide had to get out to push the boat clear again. Once or twice, we thought we might have to get out and push as well." We asked if they had seen any birds, insects or animals and Shelagh described some of the very brightly coloured butterflies that had come down in swarms to drink from the muddy pools at the water's edge.

In the meantime, the rest of us were given the opportunity to fish from the side of the ship and we caught several piranha. One of the American girls, Bobby (pronounced "Barby"), caught a walking catfish and Moazir brought it round the ship so that we could all see it before it was returned to the river.

The usual group of curious children were gathered round the ship and Ed entertained them with a few magic tricks and later decided to go swimming with them, diving straight off the side of the ship into the river. We thought this was a bit risky because although the water looked exceptionally clear at this point, it was very difficult to judge how deep it was.

Afterwards Moazir, who was a native Amazonian Indian, brought out his blowpipe for us to inspect and handle. It was about seven feet long and quite heavy and must have been difficult to aim accurately. Because of the length and weight, I found it almost impossible to hold it steady. The blowpipe is made in two halves which are then glued together and the poisoned dart is inserted at the mouth end and has to travel the whole length of the tube so it is essential that the central channel is straight and true.

This was to be our last night on board and if it was possible to improve on previous sunsets, we had the most spectacular sunset of the cruise that evening. Over dinner, Carol asked our group to pack an overnight bag before morning, holding sufficient for a night in an Amazon jungle camp and a flight to Cuzco, and to have our other cases packed and out on deck before 6.30am to be taken to Cuzco direct.

That night was party night. We were each given a free drink made of sugar cane rum and black corn, red-brown in colour and very fiery and then there was disco dancing on deck until 4am. James had met a very slim, attractive young lady who was a tour guide from Colombia, travelling alone, and he was pleased to introduce her to us. As usual, the night was perfect, warm and balmy with just enough breeze

115

to keep us cool while we danced and the time passed all too quickly.

Bobby, the American girl, who had left her husband at home and was travelling with her mother, confided to us that it was her lifelong ambition to climb Huayna Picchu, the mountain that towers behind the Inca ruins of Macchu Picchu. She had been in training for this for the past few months and hoped that she was now sufficiently fit to reach the top. We wished her all the best and said that we might see her there as our tour also went to Macchu Picchu.

At 4am, the disco was still in full swing but David and I decided we needed a brief sleep. We sorted out what was required for our overnight bag and packed the cases ready for morning before going to bed, still hearing the beat of the music in our heads.

Day 15. Saturday 17th September.

We were due to leave the ship at 7am to travel to Iquitos by open motor boat but while we were having breakfast, Dino came to tell us that a storm was brewing. It had therefore been decided that we should stay on board the cruise ship until we reached Iquitos.

When the storm struck about an hour later, we were very grateful for this decision. The rain was torrential and although part of the deck was under cover, the squalls of wind drove the rain inside so that we had to retreat to our cabins or the dining room.

Iquitos turned out to be a very large place, sprawling several miles along the banks of the Amazon, with luxury villas built on raised ground alongside clusters of palm roofed stilt huts and the occasional oil refinery. As we continued up river, the rain eased off and eventually stopped by the time we reached the far end of Iquitos where we berthed in the river next to our sister ship, El Arca.

The two ships were tied together firmly, fore and aft, and we then had to climb from our ship on to El Arca and cross that ship before going down a gangplank on to a floating jetty from which we could reach the shore. We were then faced by a very steep climb up ladders to the top of the bank about 50 feet above us. The steps of the ladders seemed to be widely spaced apart and by the time we reached the platform at the top, we were all exhausted. The lack of sleep the night before may have had something to do with it.

At the top we had a long wait while Carol, still on board the Rio Amazonas, ensured that all our baggage was unloaded. We were able to watch as the porters ran up the ladders with our suitcases, carrying up to five large cases each. These men looked thin and wiry but were superbly fit and strong. The luggage was piled up in the inner waiting room and we each ensured that our own cases were there. While we waited, we were entertained by an excellent Peruvian band who played the ubiquitous "El Condor Passa" which we heard everywhere we went in Peru. There was a collection at the end and the band probably made quite a good living from the tour ships.

Once Carol had ensured that the main luggage was safely loaded on to a van to be taken to the airport for our flight to Cuzco, we picked up our overnight bags and went through the building to the main street where a bus was waiting for us. This bus had no glass or cellophane in the windows. There was evidence that it had once been red but it appeared to have been newly painted bright yellow in our honour.

We made our way inside and sat down. Almost immediately there were cries of distress. "Oh no, this was my best T-shirt." "Look at my trousers!" Unfortunately, the bus was so newly painted that the heat of the sun had melted the paint on one side of the bus and those seated on that side stuck to their seats and had yellow paint all over their clothing. There was little Carol could do about it apart from promising to try to buy some white spirit in Cuzco. David and I thanked our lucky stars that we had sat on the shady side of the bus.

7

AMAZON CAMP

We were driven along what appeared to be a ring road around Iquitos. What we saw of the city looked very poor apart from a large concrete naval base and some factories. The driving seemed to be rather erratic and we noticed that above the driver's head were several pictures of Christ, presumably to protect him on his travels. These were surrounded by fairy lights which lit up every time the driver braked, which was frequently.

Suddenly we reached the end of the road and lurched across the mud to the Rio Nanay, a tributary of the Amazon. We were thankful to alight from the bus and escape the overpowering smell of new paint and although one or two of the party were still complaining about their spoilt clothes, the rest had accepted it as one of the experiences of the holiday.

We made our way to a small wooden landing stage and boarded a motorised canoe that would take us up the Rio Nanay and then into a smaller winding tributary on which was situated the Amazon Camp where we would be spending the next night. We passed several similar boats on the way, most of which had palm leaf shelters over them to provide shade. Our boat had no such luxury and the sun was scorching hot but after about half an hour, we arrived at the camp, in an idyllic setting on the river bank.

Clutching our overnight bags, we had to climb up a flight of steep, very slippery wooden steps with bamboo handrails. "Mind you don't fall," warned Shelagh. We then made our way along a wooden walkway raised on stilts about two feet above the ground to a large open verandah with a palm leaf roof. Behind this was the Reception area where cans of drink were available. We immediately queued for beer and cola.

Karl, Phil, Nigel and James were the first to be served. They put their glasses down on one of the small wooden tables spread around the verandah and sank into the cushioned bamboo chairs. Sipping his drink and sighing with satisfaction, James said, "I was ready for this." We soon joined them and sat relaxing on the verandah in the shade, enjoying our much-needed beers while the rooms were being allocated, before collecting our keys and making our way to our rooms, reached along the raised wooden walkways.

The bedrooms were all part of one long building with tall dividing walls. They had leaf thatch roofs and walls of bamboo up to waist height above which mosquito netting was stretched between poles to form the upper walls, allowing the air to circulate. Each room also had a bathroom which was more private, with bamboo walls to roof height, and with a toilet, washbasin and occasional running water.

We were free for the rest of the morning and I spent time watching some golden orioles in a tree near the Reception area. Their nest hung down from the branches like an untidy grassy compost heap and the birds which were a vivid golden yellow contrasting with near-black were constantly coming and going so I assumed they were feeding their young fledglings.

As I was hot and sticky, I then decided to try out the showers, reached by a walkway that led behind the bedroom areas. The shower area had a concrete floor and consisted of two rows of cubicles, those on the left for women, those on the right for men, the cubicles having shoulder-high bamboo walls, open to the sky above. The shower heads were supported by the slightly higher outer wall of the complex. The water was lovely, cool and refreshing and it felt delightful showering out in the open air.

When I rejoined the group on the verandah, Carol was there in her swimsuit. She wanted to be more adventurous and swim in the river and was trying to persuade the others to join her. The river was a yellow-brown and not particularly inviting but eventually Jack agreed to join her and went to get changed. We watched from above as they made their way down the slippery steps to the small landing stage and then dived into the river. They immediately discovered that there was a treacherous undercurrent sweeping along the shoreline and shouted to each other to climb out quickly.

Luckily they were both strong swimmers but it took all their efforts to stay in the same place and avoid being swept downstream. Jack struggled to climb back on to the landing stage and having made it, helped Carol out of the river. They both sat there for a time, safe but panting with the exertion and shock. We observers were also shocked as we realised that we could so easily have lost them both in those few seconds.

Not long afterwards, the dinner gong was sounded. The gong consisted of a beautifully carved, hollowed out log suspended from the handrail of the walkway to the dining room. When it was hit with a piece of wood, the sound reverberated surprisingly loudly. The dining room, we discovered, was down another walkway behind the Reception area. Lunch consisted of fish, rice, salad, bread, a banana and coffee and was very enjoyable.

After the meal, we were taken on a jungle walk to meet the Huitotos Indians. David, who had still not fully recovered from his bout of illness at Leticia, decided to relax in the shade on the veranda with a book.

Our new guide took us down a jungle trail and, on the way, pointed out various trees and plants and told us of their uses.

He showed us a plant known as iroke which only grows to a height of about three feet and has a crown of large spreading leaves, each about two feet long. "These leaves are used for thatching," he told us. "They are easier to pick and more manageable than palm leaves." Then, pointing to something similar to a fern, "The roots of this plant are ground to a powder to cure headaches and fever." We then saw another of the trees related to the rubber tree and he told us that, as well as being taken for indigestion, the sap can be rubbed on the skin to ease rheumatic pains and bruising.

We passed a cleared area on which a low, green crop was growing. "This is a young tapioca plantation," explained our guide. "The trees will soon grow to about five feet in height. Tapioca roots have tubers like potatoes and the village women collect these and chew them to mix them with saliva. The resulting pulp is then put into bowls and left to ferment before being used to produce the local alcoholic beverage." We mentally made a note not to try the local brew.

Bringing up the luggage at Iquitos

Amazon Camp

Huitotos dancers

Hunter with blowpipe

Selling necklaces

Further along a log had fallen across the path and was covered in moving patches of green, brown and yellow. On closer inspection, these turned out to be pieces of leaf, many times the size of the little leaf-cutting ants carrying them back to their nest. "The entrance to the nest is a hole about an inch in diameter," explained our guide. Some of the leaf pieces looked more than an inch across and I wondered if the ants would forcibly bend these to pull them inside or whether they would cut them into smaller segments.

"The pieces of leaf," our guide continued, "are used to feed a fungus which the ants grow in their nests and then the ants feed on the fungus." One of the ants had a large triangle of leaf that kept falling to one side and each time, the little ant had to exert all its strength to pull it upright again; it reminded me of a windsurfer trying to keep his sail aloft.

In a clearing, we saw what appeared to be the branch of a tree covered in small yellow blossoms and discovered that it was an orchid. We crossed several streams on log bridges and, as we drew close to the village, passed what our guide told us was an Indian graveyard among the trees, the graves being marked with boulders.

Eventually we came to a grassy clearing in the centre of which was a single shelter consisting of a leaf thatch roof supported by occasional uprights. It had no walls. A bench ran along one side of the shelter and we sat on this and waited. On the opposite side of the shelter was a tree trunk about thirty feet long supported by logs at either end, lifting the centre clear of the ground. There were a few other logs at the side and our hosts were either sitting on these, leaning against the uprights or standing around silently in small groups.

Here the small children were not kept separate from the rest of the tribe but were running around naked and very much part of the group. Three of the youngsters raced across the clearing, each holding a twig on which was impaled a single leaf that spun round as they ran, catching the wind like a European child's toy windmill.

The adult dancers and older children were dressed in cotton with a stencilled or batik design in dark brown on a white background. The women wore short skirts and tops while the men wore longer, knee-length skirts and all wore headdresses of cotton bands in a brown and white design, decorated with beautiful long feathers in a deep blue colour. One woman also had an even longer red feather in the centre of her headdress and as this particular woman also had her face decorated with black lines from her nose and the sides of her mouth, we assumed she was a person of importance.

When the performance started, we were again told that we would be seeing a spider monkey dance and an anaconda dance; however, the dances themselves were very different from those we had seen previously. In the first dance, the Indians walked round in a circle, chanting, each with a hand on the shoulder of the person in front. The children tried to follow and were generally in the way but everyone seemed to enjoy it, particularly when the tempo quickened and they all galloped in a long row out of the hut, across the clearing and back again, the children laughing and giggling.

Then came the anaconda dance. The men stood at the back of the shelter, each with one foot on the long tree trunk which was supported at either end. They thumped this up and down on the ground for the rhythm and also rattled bean pods tied to long sticks while all the Indians sang. The dancers stood in rows which weaved alternately from side to side. The youngest children stood in the front row where they were unable to see what the other dancers were doing and although they kept turning round to try to watch the others, it was not surprising that they tended to go in different directions.

The audience then joined in and again the tempo quickened until, in our alternate rows, we were all galloping sideways in and out of the shelter before stopping to catch our breath at the end of the dance. Now that we were all laughing and in a good mood, it was time to bargain for the goods hanging from the roof.

There was less choice here and the Huitotos were only interested in cash, not in exchanging goods. We all felt obliged to purchase something and I bought a hollow painted gourd with a lid and a woven strap. We then walked to the village where we saw one of the Indians with his blowpipe, again about seven feet in length with a bag of arrow tips tied to one end. Our guide borrowed it to show to us and to demonstrate its use.

The village consisted of about ten wooden huts on stilts with thatched roofs, some quite large with an outer verandah at the top of the steps, others with apparently only a single room. Some had planks of wood for the walls which indicated that there may be a sawmill nearby. A lady came over to try to sell necklaces made of nuts and seeds but by this time, we had purchased all the necklaces we required. On the way back to the camp, we spotted some huge Morpho butterflies, several inches across, whose wings were a dazzling blue when open, black when closed.

Back at base, I had another shower to cool me down and we sat on the verandah chairs as dusk fell and the hurricane lamps were lit. These lamps gave no more light that a candle but looked romantic. There was another party staying at the camp who had flown in from Cuzco and they showed us some of the souvenirs they had purchased. "Look at this," one of them said proudly. "This will cause a sensation back home." It was a huge banana spider in a glass-fronted wooden display case. The beast was more than a foot across with long, thick, hairy legs and we shuddered and hoped that we did not knowingly come too close to a live specimen.

The dinner gong sounded and we made our way to the dining room using our torches. The dining room was lit by two hurricane lamps and while this created a delightful atmosphere, it made it very difficult to see what we were eating. After the meal, we found the walkways had been lit by very occasional hurricane lamps and there was also one provided for each bedroom.

We used our torch in the bathroom, keeping the hurricane lamp in the main room. As my T-shirt was wet, I optimistically hung it up to dry overnight and went to bed in my damp trousers and a dry, clean shirt.

We had little or no sleep that night. Not long after we were in bed, there was a loud bang followed by an exclamation. Shortly after that we heard another loud bang and we lay awake wondering what on earth it could be. Then it started raining and continued throughout the night and David found that the palm leaf roof leaked directly over his bed.

"Can I help you to move the bed across?" I asked. "No, it doesn't matter now," he replied, "I'm already wet through so I might as well stay here," and he spent the rest of the night under the constant dripping from the leaves above. We could hear the staff patrolling up and down the walkways all night. David thought they were looking out for snakes and other creatures to make sure none found its way into the rooms. Then at around midnight, another group arrived, loudly chatting as they made their way to their accommodation.

Day 16. Sunday 18th September.

At 3am we had a wake-up call and found there was no water in the taps although we had some bottled water for cleaning our teeth. All our clothes were wet through, including the T-shirt that had been hung up to dry. We packed our rucksacks and took them with us to the dining room, using the torch to find our way as most of the hurricane lamps had gone out by this time and with the rain, it was completely dark.

We were provided with bread, jam and coffee which helped to bring us round. There was just one hurricane lamp to light the whole of the dining room which made it even more difficult to see what we were doing, particularly as the side table from which we were helping ourselves was hidden by our shadows. While we were eating, we discovered the reasons for the loud bangs the previous evening.

Graham was the cause of the first of these. He usually enjoyed a cigarette just before going to bed but not on this occasion. "My matches were too damp to light," he explained. "I tried to dry them out by holding them over the hurricane lamp but I accidentally dropped them all inside and nearly blew myself up." "I know about the second bang," said James. "I was just climbing into bed when the two legs at the bottom collapsed. I spent the night at an angle of 45 degrees, trying not to slide off the end."

Having eaten, we made our way back along the walkway and down the steps to the motorised canoe. The overnight rain had made the wooden steps even more slippery and we found it too difficult to hold on to bags and the handrail as well as a torch so the torches were put away and we slithered and felt our way down very gingerly in pitch darkness to the narrow landing stage and the open boat.

Carol told us later that the previous group had not bothered with the steps but had slid straight down the mud bank and into the river, holding their luggage over their heads and climbing into the canoe covered in mud and soaked to the skin. (I assume the river current had not been so strong on that occasion!) They had then washed off the mud at the airport before boarding the aircraft.

Once we were settled in the boat, we were told to extinguish all torches as they would distract the "driver" and we sped round the bends of the winding river and back to Iquitos in pitch darkness, lit only by the glimmer of the pilot's torch to show him the way.

At Iquitos, we climbed up the sloping mud bank in the dark and waited for our bus which came after a quarter of an hour. Luckily the paint was now dry and the driver took us to the airport through the centre of Iquitos.

On the journey, Carol told us that Iquitos was the largest city in the Amazon Basin with no road access, being linked to the outside world only by river or by air. "It is another settlement that grew and thrived during the 19th century rubber boom," she said, "but this was followed by a long period of decline until oil was discovered in the 1960s. This and the recent growth in tourism have both helped in the return to prosperity. Many of the buildings are decorated on the outside with Portuguese tiles imported by the rubber barons."

We could only gain a general impression of the city as we drove through because it was still dark. Then, as we pulled up at red traffic lights, a drunk climbed unsteadily on board.

"Dos de Mayo," he said to the driver in a slurred voice, holding out his fare. The driver tried to explain that this was not the local bus. The drunk stared at him, looked at us sitting in the passenger seats and looked back at the driver again, thoroughly confused. "Dos de Mayo, por favor," he tried again, a little more loudly.

In the meantime, the lights had changed and the blare of horns indicated that drivers in the traffic behind us were getting impatient. Our driver once more told the man that this was not a local bus and the guide confirmed this. The man started to look a little belligerent so Carol came down the bus, tried to calm him down and explained that the bus was on private hire and was only going to the airport. Eventually the man got off again, muttering to himself and sounding very annoyed and we continued on our way.

When we reached the airport a pan pipe band was playing but the incident with the drunk had delayed us somewhat so we were unable to stop and listen. We only just had time to collect our boarding cards before making our way to the airplane. Had we arrived covered in mud like the previous group, we certainly would have had no time to wash it off. However, we knew exactly how they felt on the flight because the rain was lashing down as we crossed the tarmac and the tropical storm soaked us through by the time we climbed on board. The air conditioning made the aircraft quite chilly and we spent the journey in cold, wet clothes, gradually drying out.

8

CUZCO AND MACCHU PICCHU

At 8am, we arrived at Cuzco, situated at a height of over 11,000 feet. At that time of the morning, the temperature was only 40° Fahrenheit and although by this time our clothes had dried out, it still felt really cold after the heat of the Amazon. We soon began to discover the effects of the altitude when we found that even the slight exertion of carrying our cases out to the coach left us breathless and gasping for air.

As we were driven from the airport, Carol took on her role of tour guide to inform us that Cuzco is the oldest continuously inhabited city on the American continent. "It was founded in the 12th century by Manco Capac, the first of the Incas and Son of the Sun," she said. "Cuzco means 'navel of the earth' in the language of the Quechua Indians who are the direct descendants of the Incas, and this city was once the centre of the Incan Empire. There is now very little evidence of Incan occupation within the city itself because after the Spaniards conquered Cuzco in 1533, they used the Incan buildings of Cuzco for the foundations for their own city. The Cathedral was actually built on the site of an old Incan palace."

We were taken straight to our hotel which was only a few minutes walk from the city centre. It was situated in a street of terraced buildings with Spanish-style roofs of curved terracotta tiles and plastered walls painted in delicate pastel shades. Terracotta pots of flowers hung outside the windows which were covered with decorative iron grilles.

Inside, the hotel resembled a medieval castle with thick white plastered walls that looked as though they were made of stone, heavy metal studded wooden doors and ceiling beams, a wide curving stone staircase and no heating whatsoever.

"While your rooms are being sorted out," said Carol, "the management would like to offer you some coca tea. This is supposed to be the most effective way of counteracting altitude sickness." We found that the drinking of coca tea is encouraged by the Government which seems strange when it is made from the same plant as cocaine which is illegal.

We were shown through to the ground floor breakfast room where we were each served with a glass of hot liquid in which floated some brown leaves. It tasted quite pleasant and we sipped it slowly and relaxed until our rooms were ready. We were then allowed just a few minutes to change into thicker trousers, jumpers and anoraks before being hurried back on to the coach for an excursion to the Sunday Market at Pisac.

When we reached the centre of Cuzco, our driver stopped to allow us to change our money. He tooted his horn and about ten money changers rushed up to the coach door, the first two being allowed on board. Carol checked with them first. "They aren't offering a very good rate," she warned us. However, we all needed Peruvian money to spend in the market and as it was Sunday, there were no banks open, so most of us exchanged some of our travellers cheques.

We travelled to Pisac, 32 km from Cuzco, on a spectacular route across the mountains. On the way, we stopped at a small market by the roadside situated high above the Urubamba valley. Below us the blue-grey river, sacred to the Incas, flowed through a narrow flat valley of greeney-brown fields surrounded by steep, abruptly rising hillsides while, in the distance, lowering clouds were caught on the peaks of the snow-capped mountains. The market consisted of half a dozen stalls displaying bright woven shawls, woollen wall hangings, bags, hats and jackets while a multitude of small items were laid out on blankets beside the road. The goods on sale were very colourful and varied but what really tempted David and me was - a packet of chocolate cream biscuits. Our last meal had been at 3am, we had not eaten anything for about seven hours and we were ravenous. We purchased the biscuits, devoured the whole packet between us and felt much better.

After this short break, we continued on our way along the road above the valley, and it was not long before we caught our first sight of Pisac far below us, an area of blue awnings indicating the site of the market. We followed the road down into the town and made for the parking area which was packed with cars and coaches.

Once the driver had managed to find a space for our coach, about a mile from the market square, we were allowed three hours to look around and have lunch. The market had spread all along the cobbled streets leading to the car and coach parks. These streets had a drainage channel running down the centre and were lined with colourful stalls on either side.

We thought that the visitors to the market were even more interesting. Locals come to the weekly market from miles around, many dressed in traditional clothing, each Indian tribe having its own particular costume.

Roadside market

Looking down on Pisac

Pisac Sunday Market

Pisac Sunday Market

Baby carrier

Pisac

Many of the women wore brightly-coloured knitwear, usually in red or blue, over full, colourfully patterned skirts, held out by voluminous, many-layered petticoats. Most wore bowler hats in various shades of brown and cream but we saw one tribe wearing circular hats supported above the head like mortar-boards, each covered with what appeared to be black velvet with a coloured design in the centre-top, the velvet edged with gold fringing which hung down to the hairline at the front and partly covered the ears at the side. From under each woman's headgear hung long dark thick plaits of hair. Many women carried young children on their backs in woven, striped, brightly-coloured blankets tied across their shoulders. The only local males we saw in the market were young boys helping to sell their wares.

As we made our way towards the main square, we noticed a large number of people wandering in and out of a courtyard. Being curious, we went inside and found a huge oven where they were baking bread. People were buying their loaves freshly baked, straight from the oven.

The stalls we passed in this part of town sold mainly smaller items such as jewellery, beads and bootlaces, vividly painted wooden chess sets and children's clothing, although there were also pullovers and wall hangings. Eventually, we reached the main market square, a colourful, seething mass of people. Foodstuffs were at one end of the market, either in sacks or spread out on cloths on the ground. All kinds of grains, nuts and vegetables were for sale plus fruit such as oranges, apples and bananas; we saw no meat or livestock. Alpaca sweaters were piled high on stalls with fabrics hung up before and behind them.

We decided to eat before the serious shopping started. We walked through a café on one side of the square and at the back, found a sunny courtyard, a haven of peace after the hubbub outside. We found that the altitude was beginning to affect our appetites and although we were hungry, one main course shared between us was more than sufficient. While we ate, a lady sharing our table proudly showed us her purchases. We then returned to the noise and bustle of the market to find our own treasures.

We had already decided to buy an alpaca sweater each but wanted to see what was available before making a choice. We were also tempted to buy some paintings by one particular artist who had some beautiful and very evocative pictures of Indians and llamas. We met Shelagh who bought two of his paintings, one depicting two llama heads and one showing three. "These will look just perfect in my house in Winnipeg," she enthused. We tried to imagine them in any of our rooms at home but as we could not think where to put them, decided against buying any in the end.

The quality and softness of the alpaca wool varied considerably from one stall to another. "Baby alpaca", insisted each and every stallholder, trying to convince us that they only had the best and we soon found that it was essential to feel the softness and texture of any sweater that we liked. They seemed to like it when we scornfully said, "No, that **must** be Grandmother alpaca" and grinned cheerfully at us.

David was the first to find what he wanted, a beautiful soft pullover in a black and white design that the stallholder admitted was brushed "Mama" alpaca. I also saw one I liked but not in my size and although the stallholder checked with her friends on another stall, they were unable to help either. Eventually, I found another sweater in cream, brown and beige, soft, warm and lovely, and after some bargaining, it was mine.

We rejoined our coach at the time arranged and were back in Cuzco by 5pm. As the sun went down, there was an instant drop in temperature. David and I walked into town to eat. We were feeling hungry but the altitude was having an increasing effect on our digestive systems. We ordered a quarter of a small pizza between us but our stomachs were so bloated with air that we could only manage a few mouthfuls each and had to leave the rest.

Back at the hotel, we were looking forward to a shower as we had been promised hot water that evening. We optimistically turned on the taps but found that the water was icy cold so we made do with a quick wash instead. We were later told that the hot tank held enough water for two people to shower and there were about sixty guests staying in the hotel.

After dark, the temperature in the hotel dropped below freezing and when we went to bed, we had to put on extra clothing, including ski pants, gloves, extra jumpers and a hat each and we then snuggled together in one single bed to try to get warm enough to sleep. Brrrhh!!

Day 17. Monday 19th September.

By testing the water on and off throughout the night, David managed to have a hot shower at 5am the next morning but although I went into the shower immediately after him, the water was already cold again. However, as we discovered later in the morning when we met the others, we were more fortunate than Carol and Nigel who were in adjoining single rooms.

"When I touched the tap, I got an electric shock that nearly threw me across the room," complained Nigel. "It's a good thing that I had bottled water to clean my teeth." "I know what you mean," confirmed Carol. "Both my taps were 'live.' I'm afraid I screamed and my arm still feels numb from last night. Did anyone else have the same problem?" Luckily the rest of us could use our water safely so Carol put in a complaint to the management on behalf of herself and Nigel.

At 6am, David and I walked into town for breakfast and Shelagh joined us at a little café on the main square. We managed a cup of hot coca tea and half a slice of toast each and, as the morning excursion did not start until 9.30am, we then had some time to explore Cuzco. The city has great character and charm. Most of the roads are cobbled and most of the buildings date back to the 16th and 17th centuries. We found two main squares, edged with buildings with arcades, some of the windows above the arcades having ornate balconies, boxed-in at the top and bottom.

The Cathedral is a very imposing building overlooking the Plaza de Armas, the square nearest to our hotel but in our opinion La Compañia is even more impressive. This is a magnificent baroque church on the same square, which we mistook for the Cathedral until Carol told us otherwise.

Wandering along to the next square, David was delighted to see a shoeshine boy. "I'm going to have my shoes cleaned," he said. As my shoes also looked grubby, I had them cleaned as well so we returned to the hotel looking quite smart. Here we found most of our group were suffering from the effects of altitude in one way or another. Most of us were feeling dizzy, lightheaded or had headaches, one or two had lost their appetites and Jean had pins and needles down her arm. Carol assured us that this was all perfectly normal. "You only need worry if your lips and finger nails turn blue," she said. "Then you must let me know immediately."

By 9.30am, we set off on our morning excursion with a local guide to see some of the Inca ruins in the vicinity of Cuzco. The temperature was rising and we soon found that in the sun we were warm enough in T-shirts although if a cloud blew across, it was instantly chilly. We made our way out of the city by coach on a steep road that zigzagged up the mountainside giving wonderful views across the city to the hills beyond.

At the top of the mountain was Sacsayhuaman fortress, the first stop on our tour. Our guide delighted in telling us that the pronunciation is very much like "sexy woman!" We left the coach and as we were not yet acclimatised, we walked around very slowly.

We were told that in Inca times, the valley at the back of the fortress had been a vast lake. Only a small part of the original structure now remains, the Spaniards having used many of the stones to construct buildings in Cuzco, but what is left is very impressive.

Our guide told us that Cuzco was originally built in the shape of a puma, an animal sacred to the Incas, with Sacsayhuaman as its head; however, try as we might, we were unable to visualise this. The main fortification has high zigzag walls, the zigzags apparently representing the teeth of the puma.

The stones of the walls lean inwards which has helped them to withstand earthquakes and although they are all different shapes and sizes, they are fitted together so tightly that it is impossible to force a knife blade between them. The corner stones are up to 10 metres high and the largest is 22 metres across. One stone alone weighs more than 300 tons and the mind boggles at the thought of transporting these huge rocks to the top of the hill, carving them accurately to shape and lifting them into position with only the crudest of tools plus human strength and ingenuity. Apparently there were once three towers above these ramparts and the garrison behind housed an army of about 5,000 men.

"Sacsayhuaman was the site of a bitter battle between the Spaniards and the Indians," our guide advised us. "In the 16th century, the conquering Spaniards under Francisco Pizarro captured Cuzco, murdered the Inca ruler and appointed a puppet Inca called Manco to do their bidding."

"After a couple of years, Manco was feeling used and aggrieved. He decided the only solution was to try to recover power for his own people by driving the Spaniards from his empire. He raised a huge army, estimated at more than 100,000 strong, laid siege to the Spaniards in Cuzco and nearly defeated them." Our guide warmed to his tale, adding expressive hand movements to emphasise what he was telling us. "Unfortunately for Manco, the Spaniards managed to break out of Cuzco and fought a violent battle at Sacsayhuaman. The clubs, spears and arrows of the Indians were no match for armoured Spaniards on horseback using swords and muskets and there was a massacre. While Manco survived, retreating first to his fortress at Ollentaytambo and then into the jungle at Vilcabamba, most of his army was killed. The thousands of dead littering the site attracted huge numbers of carrion-eating condors. This is why, to this day, you will see eight condors included in Cuzco's coat of arms."

The excitement of the story and the thin atmosphere had made us very thirsty and we were glad of our bottled water. We climbed some steps through a stone archway and ascended the hill against which the wall was built. At the top was a circular structure and Shelagh, who had something of the mystic in her, stood in the centre with her arms raised to the heavens, trying to sense the energy fields emanating from the stones. Our guide hurried us on before she had a chance to do so.

Plaza de Armas, Cuzco

Sacsayhuaman fortress

143

Stone circle at Sacsayhuaman

Qenko Temple

From the top of the hill, we could see Cuzco lying below and further along the escarpment, a statue of Christ stood on a small mound, overlooking and protecting the city. In the opposite direction, we looked across from the top of the ramparts to Rodadero Hill, a long low hill with large pieces of natural rock on its flanks and at one end, four stone platforms or benches tiered one above the other and known as the throne of the Inca.

Between the two hills was the large flat area across which we had entered the site which, we were told, had an important religious as well as military significance for the Incas. "The level ground between the two hills is used on 24 June each year for the Inti Raymi," explained our guide. "This is a re-enactment of an Inca festival which attracts thousands of tourists annually. You really should try to attend this if you possibly can." Down in Cuzco, we had seen leaflets advertising this event in which hundreds take part, dressed in Inca costume. We all wanted to see this wonderful spectacle.

Unfortunately, while we stood looking down on this level area, a group of police started roaring around on motorbikes. "They are here to protect the ruins from vandalism," we were told. While the police may have been a deterrent, we privately thought that any vandals up in the ruins would have been able to continue with their desecration undetected had they wished to do so. As it was, the police completely ruined the atmosphere.

On the way back to the coach, we saw a lady in traditional Peruvian costume holding two llamas on ropes. She wore a very full black skirt with a red hem, a red jacket with black reveres and a circular hat, its black and red segments separated by narrow white strips. She looked very smart and was happy to pose for photographs for a small charge. "This is not begging," our guide assured us. "At official tourist sites, local people see this as a legitimate and honourable form of income as they are offering their services as professional models."

Our next visit was to Tambo Machay, a temple for the worship of the water god. A spring flowing through the temple was known as the Water of Eternal Life and a ceremonial stone bath in the temple is known as El Baño del Inca. Because of its purity, the water from this spring was once used to make the local Cuzco beer.

From here, we were taken to a souvenir shop miles from anywhere, where our guide was obviously hoping to earn commission. We had seen better quality and cheaper goods in the Sunday market at Pisac so we waited outside and looked at a passing herd of what we thought were all llamas.

As we set off again, our guide explained that while the larger animals were llamas, the slightly smaller, woollier animals were alpacas. "There is also a larger member of the same family, the guanaco, and a smaller member, the vicuña," he said. "Most of these animals are kept for their wool rather than their meat." David and I were pleased that we had now seen the kind of animals which had supplied the wool for our new sweaters.

The next site we visited was Qenko, the temple of the puma god. A large rock in the centre of a square altar was said to be shaped like a puma but again it required a great deal of imagination to visualise this. Between some jagged rocks, a fissure led to a small cave containing a stone altar which, our guide told us, was used by the Incas for human sacrifices. A mummified figure had been discovered in the cave and it was thought that this may once have been a high priestess.

Above the cave, steps led to the top of the rugged limestone rocks which had zigzag channels cut into them. Qenko means "zigzag" and it was these channels that gave the site its name although their purpose is unclear, one suggestion being that they were used to drain blood from the sacrifices.

Fortunately, this was the last site of our tour. Most of our group managed to climb to the top of the limestone rocks but I no longer had enough energy for this and was glad to return to the hotel where I collapsed on the bed with a fever.

David and I decided to skip the included afternoon city tour as we had already seen much of the town centre. After a couple of hours in a horizontal position, I felt much better and we walked into town for a late lunch of half a toasted sandwich each.

It had been suggested that we should buy a picnic for the following day when we were going to visit Macchu Picchu. We found this quite difficult as the supermarkets tended to sell things in bulk. Eventually we managed to find a store selling pre-packed sandwiches. We took it very easy in the afternoon and that evening, our main meal consisted of a bowl of hot tomato soup each as we were simply unable to eat any more. Back at the hotel, we packed an overnight bag plus water, sandwiches and the camera equipment and had an early night.

Day 18. Tuesday 20th September.

The following morning we were up at 4am and actually **both** achieved a hot shower. Luxury! Early breakfast was laid on at the hotel and I managed a whole slice of toast with my coca tea before we left with our overnight bags at 5am. We went by bus to Cuzco station and changed to another bus with very narrow seats and no space for luggage. This bus took us to Ollentaytambo bus station, the last ten minutes of the journey being on a rough dirt road.

It was then only a short walk to the railway station where we joined the train to Macchu Picchu. Having found our reserved seats on the train, we went to investigate the different items being sold by the Indians who were standing all over the rail tracks holding up their wares to tempt the rich tourists. Phil and I each bought a Macchu Picchu T-shirt. After about fifteen minutes, the tracks were cleared, we resumed our seats and we set off by train down the beautiful valley of the Urubamba, Sacred River of the Incas.

As the train followed the course of the river between the mountains, catering staff brought round complimentary coca tea or black coffee plus sandwiches containing cheese and ham and they sold guide books in many different languages. We were also able to watch a video of the site if we wished.

We left the train at Puente Ruinas, the station closest to the ruins, and joined the queue for one of the buses ferrying people up the mountain on a narrow zigzag road, the Hiram Bingham Road, which was being repaired in several places where it had crumbled away. There was no sign of the ruins from this point. We were soon on the bus which climbed the road through the forest for a distance of about six kilometres and stopped outside a hotel at the top of the hill.

Carol arranged for us to leave our overnight bags at Reception and we set off along the road to the ruins. Although we were now on a level with these, we could still see very little of them as they were almost hidden by a perimeter wall and a row of huts up the side of the hill. These were the watchtower huts guarding the entrance.

The city of Macchu Picchu was once an important ceremonial centre and nobody knows for certain why it was deserted. Some think it was destroyed by the Incas before they fled from the Spaniards in the early 16th century although the Spaniards never found this particular site. Others think Macchu Picchu was deserted long before the Spanish conquest. Whatever the reason, it remained hidden and unknown until July 1911 when it was discovered by the American explorer, Hiram Bingham.

The buildings were completely covered by vegetation in the middle of a dense forest and since the discovery, there has been an ongoing effort to clear the site and reconstruct the buildings. Builders were working at the lower end of the city while we were there.

As we were on a group ticket, we all went through the entrance gate together and entered the city along the agricultural terraces via one of the watchtowers, a stone building with a palm-thatched roof. Carol then presented us with various options.

"This afternoon," she said, "you may like to come with me on a walk along the Inca trail as far as the Intipunku or Sun Gate from where travellers on the Inca Trail first glimpsed the city. We shall be returning here tomorrow morning when you can either join me on a climb to the top of Huayna Picchu, the triangular shaped mountain towering over the ruins, or take a guided tour through the ruins. If anyone wants to do both, you should miss breakfast and catch an early bus. If you start the climb early enough, there may be time to tour the ruins as well although it would be wise to ask the guide to make it a very brief tour."

The altitude here was only about 7,500 feet, much lower than at Cuzco, and I had immediately begun to feel the benefit of this but David was still suffering and completely lacking in energy so we decided to take our time exploring the ruins. Carol told us when the group was to meet outside the hotel to take the bus back down into the valley and she set off at a brisk pace with most of the party following.

David and I took our time, drinking in the splendour of the ruins and the beauty of the site. As we wandered round, we kept meeting up with different groups and their official guides and thus learnt something about the buildings we passed. Although we had not paid for their services, the guides were all very friendly and welcomed us as temporary members of their parties. We made our way along the Central Plaza, the wide flat area that divides the city into upper and lower halves and at the far end, found where the footpath started for the ascent of Huayna Picchu.

Turning back to the city, we climbed steps up to the higher part of the city on the right where we stopped at the sacristy, a building where three of the walls still stood and where the upper part of the central wall had seven niches in the top row of stones, probably used for storing ceremonial objects. All the walls leant inwards slightly to give them strength and the stones were again carved so exactly that a knife blade would not fit between the joints; however, at one end, the central wall had sunk and the stones had been pulled apart, perhaps due to earthquake damage. The guide here said that the two huge stones on either side of the entrance each had 32 angles but we did not attempt to count them.

Behind the sacristy, steps led up a narrow hill and we followed these up, between supporting walls and through a stone doorway, to a small platform on top of the hill. Here we found an intriguing stone carved into many different levels and angles surmounted by what appeared to be a small "trig point" pillar with a sloping upper surface. Another guide told us that this was the Intihuatana, a Quechuan word meaning "hitching post of the sun", used as the main shrine and also an astronomical observatory.

"The four corners of the top pillar indicate the four points of the compass," the guide up here informed us. "Inca astronomers used different angles of the construction to predict the solstices of the sun, enabling the Inca, the Son of the Sun, to tell his people exactly when the days would start to lengthen again for the return of summer. At one time, all important Inca sites would have had an Intihuatana but the Spaniards destroyed all those that they found because they thought they were used for sun worship and therefore blasphemous."

Taking a path down the other side of the hill, we arrived back at the Central Plaza and from here, made our way towards the agricultural terraces and up some steps on the right to the "Hut of the Caretaker of the Funerary Rock". This is the place from which all the travel brochure photographs of Macchu Picchu are taken. There is a perfect view across the site from this point, high above the city which is situated on an almost flat plateau, protected at the far end by the towering bulk of Huayna Picchu and on the left side by a much smaller triangular buttress. On either side, there is an almost vertical drop to the valley below while the snow-capped Andes mountains tower on the far side of the encircling valley. This impregnable site would have caught all the sunshine available while being protected from the worst of the weather.

There was a seat in the "Hut of the Caretaker..." and David was feeling really tired so we stopped here to rest and eat our sandwiches. Two of the Inca trails started from this point and I was longing to explore so, having promised to return within one hour, I left David chatting to other visitors to the hut and set off on a trail to the right, leading to the Inca Drawbridge.

The path was an attractive narrow rocky trail round the edge of the hillside with spectacular views between the rocky outcrops to the sacred Urubamba Valley, a dizzying near-vertical drop below. After only twenty minutes walking, however, there was a barrier across the path. Looking beyond this, it was possible to see a wide gap where the drawbridge would have been. On the other side of the gap, the path continued as a very steep, very narrow flight of steps clinging to the slightly overhanging cliff face with a vertical drop below. With no handrail, it would have needed a very good head for heights to even attempt to negotiate these.

I returned to tell David what I had seen and then, having agreed a further hour and a half, set off to explore the Inca trail to the left which led to the Intipunku, the Gate of the Sun, and eventually all the way to Cuzco.

To start with, the stone pathway was quite wide with a stone wall to the right and vegetation to the left and the occasional llama watching curiously from the grass terraces on the right as I walked past. Further along, the trail became very narrow with a vertical wall of rock to the right and the mountain falling away steeply on the left. A rope attached to the rock wall provided some security but having to pass walkers coming from the opposite direction presented quite a problem.

Those on the inside had to flatten themselves against the rock face, holding on to the rope, while those on the outside edged past them, clutching them around the waist for protection until they could grab hold of the rope again. Luckily I only met one person on this stretch who was happy to pass me on the outside.

It soon became evident that I would have insufficient time to reach the Intipunku but I did reach an excellent viewpoint from where I could see the Hiram Bingham Road, which we had ascended by bus, zigzagging up from the valley below.

Macchu Picchu from the Hut of the Caretaker of the Funerary Rock

Macchu Picchu

153

View of the ruins

I did it! On top of Huayna Picchu

As I made my way back, storms rumbled round the surrounding mountains and lightning flashed but Macchu Picchu remained bathed in sunshine the whole time. It was easy to imagine how inspirational the sight would have been to someone who had endured the hardships of travelling through the mountains for several days and then had suddenly seen Macchu Picchu for the first time as he came through the Intipunku.

By the time I got back to David, he was cold and bored as the other visitors had left the hut some time before, but he welcomed me without complaint. We still had a little while left to explore the ruins and we came down past the Temple of the Sun, the only circular building in the city. This was roped off as work was being carried out on it but we were told that its oddly shaped window was called the Serpent Window - we never found out why! A flight of steps led down from the other side of the temple to the ceremonial baths, from where water could be seen running in a channel from the upper to the lower part of the city, from one small pool to another. Below this was the prison area. We had a short time to wander around in the lower part of the city before it was time to make our way back to the hotel, collect our belongings, meet the rest of our party and board the bus.

As we descended the mountain on the Hiram Bingham Road, we gradually became aware of a small boy aged about twelve, who waved to the bus and whooped loudly as it passed before he disappeared into the trees beside the road. As we came round the next long bend, there he was, waiting for us, ready to wave and whoop again.

We soon started looking out for him as we rounded each bend and sure enough, there he was, waving and whooping to us all the way to the bottom where he boarded the bus and was well rewarded for his efforts. He wore a pullover that proclaimed he was a Chaska Boy, messenger of the gods. He told us that he ran down the mountain four times a day so we considered he had earned his money. Steve had a video camera and as he filmed, the Chaska Boy whooped for him so he obviously knew that the video camera also recorded sound. Carol told us that the Chaskas ran along the mountain trails carrying messages from one Inca community to another.

We stayed on the bus beyond Puente Ruinas to a village further down the valley called Aguas Calientes, famous for its hot springs and tightly ringed by mountains. On arrival, we crossed the railway line and a small square in the bottom of the valley to reach a long street of steps. This took us up to the Youth Hostel where we were staying, about halfway up the street.

We entered a very spacious reception hall behind which was a small garden area with a little shrine and accommodation blocks which held twin bedrooms and communal areas with showers, washbasins and toilets. The rooms were modern, and clean if somewhat spartan and we were promised hot water after 9pm.

At 6.30pm, Carol invited us to join her on a visit to the hot baths at the top of the street. Although we had no swimsuits in our overnight bag, we were curious to see the baths and it was an opportunity to see where the restaurants were located on the way. It seemed a long climb up the steps and we were tired and breathless by the time we reached the top of the street which ended at the entrance to the baths, calling themselves the "Baños del Inca".

The street lights also ended here and we wished we had brought the torch as the paved street gave way to a stony footpath with only an occasional hurricane lamp to indicate the direction we should take. The path led up beside a mountain stream with waterfalls but although we could hear them, we were unable to make them out in the dark.

At the top of the path was an illuminated concrete area with a bar, changing rooms and the main bath, the size of a small swimming pool. This bath was full of bodies, most of whom turned out to be a group who had been walking the Inca trail from Cuzco and had camped out every night on the trail. This was their first opportunity to wash for four days and they were luxuriating in the hot water and enjoying every minute of it.

From the baths, David and I made our way down the hill to a rustic-looking restaurant where we ordered tomato soup and bread with papaya juice to drink. In the restaurant were two rather noisy yellow and blue macaws, a four-piece band to entertain us and a large open clay wood-burning oven where most of the food was cooked. Soon after we had ordered, the other group arrived, exuberant after their hot bath, and joined us. They all ordered pizzas which were cooked in the bottom of the oven, the blazing wood having been pushed to one side. After the meal, a couple of them danced with the owner's small son, aged about six, who had limitless enthusiasm and energy.

The group was camping out again that night and left shortly after 9pm to erect their tents on a site down beside the river. We were glad to be staying in the hostel, even though the promised hot water never materialised.

Day 19. Wednesday 21st September.

We left the hostel at 7.15am the next morning. The shaving points had failed to work so most of the men were looking rather rough and stubbly and many of the party were suffering from diarrhoea and looking washed-out. However, by the time we had taken the bus up the mountain to Macchu Picchu and eaten a hot breakfast in the hotel at the top, most of us felt much better and fit to tackle Huayna Picchu.

At the bottom of the mountain, the bus had stopped to pick up a dozen "Chaska Boys", all about the same size and dressed identically. It dropped them off at various points all the way up the mountain and we now knew exactly how the scam worked. However, it had provided us with amusement and nobody begrudged what we had paid the previous day.

David decided to stay in the hotel and relax while I joined Carol as she led us through the ruins for the start of the walk. As I panted breathlessly along behind the rest of the party, I soon realised I would be unable to keep up and decided to slow down and do the climb at my own pace.

I stopped to take a few photographs and the rest of the party were soon out of sight. The ascent of Huayna Picchu began with a steep descent over a fairly narrow strip of land with a rope to stop people falling over the edge. As I arrived at this point, I met Steve and Betty who had turned back as neither had a good head for heights.

I was fine going downhill but after a narrow flattish area, steps climbed steeply up the other side and I found I could only climb about ten steps before I was out of breath. Every few yards, I sat down panting and admired the scenery until I felt able to continue again. I caught up with an American party that was even slower than I was but they had all day to do the climb. After about ten minutes with them, I decided that I would run out of time and be unable to reach the top unless I went on alone.

When I had been climbing for about an hour, I met Shelagh on her way back down. She told me I was nearly halfway but warned me about a mudslide up ahead. She had skipped breakfast and set off alone before the rest of the party but had been held up at the slide until two Australians had arrived and helped her up. She had also needed help right at the top. I reached the slide a little further on. The path, at an angle of 45°, was smooth and slippery and from this it was necessary to climb up on to a rock about three feet high. As soon as I raised one foot to climb up, I slid back down the slope. After a few unsuccessful attempts, I was helped up by a Japanese couple on their way back down.

Further on, the path divided, those going up the mountain being directed to a path off to the right which led to a small plateau with wonderful views down to Macchu Picchu and the Hiram Bingham Road. Above this, steps led up to a steep narrow tunnel through the rock.

In the centre of the tunnel, it was too dark to see the steps and the roof of the tunnel was too low for me to wear my rucksack which I had to push up the steps in front of me. It was quite exciting!

From here, the climb was straightforward until I was nearly at the top when, like Shelagh, I again needed assistance. A Chilean couple took my camera and rucksack while I pushed with hands and feet against one rock and my back against another rock to work my way up to the top of a third rock which was shoulder high. Eventually I reached the summit where a Spaniard took my photograph, triumphantly perched on a triangle of rock with my back to the sheer drop down to Macchu Picchu far below.

I then faced the descent. A group of Spaniards helped me over the first obstacle, a huge, smooth rock face sloping downwards at an angle of 45° and about fifteen feet across. As I started down it, I felt as though I would tumble head first into space as I was looking straight into the valley below. I inched down very slowly, pigeon-toed, while the Spaniards waited for me and encouraged me. I found out afterwards that our group had sat down here and shuffled across the slab on their bottoms. Below this was a steep, rough area but a rope was provided along the cliff face which helped me to keep my balance and stay on my feet.

Further down, I came to a run of very steep steps, covering a drop of about twenty feet, where the depth of each step was less than the width of a shoe. I took this very slowly, leaning in towards the steps and crossing one foot over the other, sideways, until I reached a more level area. From here there was a view across to the plateau where a group of people, still on their way to the top, were taking photographs.

A little further on, the paths joined again and on the way down, I was able to help another couple up the mud slide. Eventually I reached the bottom. It had taken me an hour and forty five minutes to reach the top and a further forty five minutes to come back down. I was later told that James had reached the top in only thirty five minutes.

I was left with a sense of exhilaration, achievement and an appreciation of the international co-operation and camaraderie extended by all those I met along the way.

Back at the hotel, I had an unhealthy lunch of crisps and cola with David and then returned to the ruins for a short time. One of the workmen showed me the plans they were using to reconstruct the site, each stone being numbered. He then tried to sell me an "Inca relic" which I politely declined.

All too soon, we were back at Puente Ruinas station (where we could have bought a hairy banana spider in a case) and we took the train and bus back to Cuzco for another cold night in our hotel. That night I had hot scrambled egg on toast for my main meal - delicious!

9

PUNO AND THE ALTIPLANO

Day 20. Thursday 22nd September.

I was up half the night with food poisoning but at least we had hot water at midnight. As we had been warned there would be no showers or baths at our next destination, Puno, I washed my hair and immediately put on my woolly hat to avoid getting pneumonia while it dried. It looked dreadful the next morning but at least it felt clean. Luckily, Carol had told us the previous evening that our 6.30am flight had been cancelled and we had been transferred to a flight at 9.30am so there was no rush to pack in the early hours.

Taking off from Cuzco was quite an experience. The aircraft seemed to take forever to leave the ground because the atmosphere is so thin; we were certain we would never rise off the runway in time. Even when airborne, we took ages to gain height. We landed at Juliaca on the Altiplano at a height of about 12,500 feet. From here, we took a bus to Sillustani, known for its chullpas or burial towers which Carol told us were pre-Incan.

These towers were built on a small hill behind a lake, Lake Umayo, and could be seen from several miles away across the flat, bleak landscape. "The chullpas were used by the Colla tribe to bury family groups with food and belongings for their journey into the next world," Carol informed us. "The only way into the towers was a small hole facing east, just large enough for a person to crawl inside, which was sealed after the burial." Although we were not told as much, we were given the impression that if the head of the family died, the rest of the family was either murdered or buried alive with him in the tower.

Although there are many chullpas in the area, those at Sillustani are the most impressive being up to 12 metres high, either round or square. They are constructed of massive blocks of stone, some decorated with carvings, in different shades of beige, brown and slate-grey which are shaped to fit together like a jigsaw puzzle; however, the edges are not flush but jut out beyond the stone courses above or below them, giving the towers an unusual shape and character. The extra altitude was affecting me and I simply did not have the energy to climb the hill and wander round the site with the rest of the group. I could see quite clearly the tower closest to where the coach was parked so I photographed that and the nearby plant life, including a lovely spiny cactus with bright red flowers. I was told afterwards that all I had really missed seeing was a ramp for levering pre-carved blocks into the correct position.

We then continued our drive across the Altiplano meaning "high plain" which, as Graham pointed out, was very high and very plain. The soil was arid and bare apart from the occasional tuft of yellow grass although in the distance, we could see trees growing at the foot of low hills where presumably they had some protection from the wind. The occasional houses were mainly single storey with few, if any, windows but with blue doors which gave a little colour to the drab landscape.

We eventually reached Puno and checked into our hotel at 3.15pm. Again there was no heating but the hotel looked more modern and the beds were comfortable. Fifteen minutes later, the group had to leave for the Floating Islands tour on Lake Titicaca as it would be dark by 6pm. I felt dizzy and exhausted so David went on the tour while I collapsed on the bed.

An hour later, I heard a band playing in the distance. By this time, having been horizontal for a while, I was feeling much better. I looked out of the window but could see nothing unusual so putting on my warmest clothes, I rushed outside. Three women were waiting by the hotel doorway to sell their blankets and wall hangings but I indicated that I was in a hurry to see the band and followed the sound. About two streets away, I was in time to see a procession of about thirty children in fancy dress costumes, mostly dressed as rabbits, ducks and elves, walking along behind a small band playing pan pipes, cymbals and drums.

We had been told that the people in this area hate being photographed so I asked permission and one proud mother, whose child was dressed as a rabbit, told me that the procession was to welcome the Spring, this being the last day of Winter. After the procession, the children would be attending a party.

At the back of the procession, a small girl was dressed as the Spring Queen, the equivalent of our May Queen. This tot, balancing on a chair in the back of an open lorry, her feet nowhere near the floor, wore a lacy white dress with a red fur-edged robe around her shoulders and a crown on her head. She waved regally to the crowd, mainly made up of parents and younger siblings.

On either side of her stood a small boy in a black dinner jacket, white shirt and red bow tie while in front were two small girls, each in a frilly pink dress with puff sleeves and white lacy collar and with a large pink rose in her hair. The sides of the lorry were hung with woollen blankets to protect the children from the cold wind, there was a lace canopy over the queen's head and from the back of the lorry, hiding the wheels, hung a red cloth decorated with dwarfs and a Disney toadstool. The whole scene was enchanting.

As I was now up and about, I decided to explore the town in what was left of the daylight. I walked up to a very impressive stone archway, its base straddling the entire pavement on either side and towering about 50 feet above the cobbled roadway. I was informed that this was built in honour of Peruvians who had died in the last century in battles for independence from the Spaniards. There was no traffic on the road but crowds of people were walking through the arch in both directions.

I then walked back down the main street, most of which was dug up and looked like a building site, and into the main square with tiled pathways, gardens protected by wrought iron railings and the equivalent of Nelson's Column in the centre. On one side was a beautiful blue and white church with something distinctly mosque-like in its architecture. By now, however, the light was fading so I returned to the hotel.

Back at the hotel, I did not have long to wait for the return of the rest of the party who had all enjoyed their trip to the floating islands. These islands are made of tortora reeds growing in Lake Titicaca. The Uros Indians began living on the reed islands many centuries ago to protect themselves firstly from the Collas and then from the Incas and their lifestyle is totally dependent on the tortora reed.

"The reed layers which make the islands are replaced on top as they rot from underneath," David told me as he was getting ready for the evening meal. "The reeds feel quite soft and springy underfoot but we had to watch where we were walking because they were spongy in places so, as we trod on them, our feet sank down into the water. Everything on the islands was made of reeds," he added. "The buildings had reed walls and reed furniture and even the fishing boats were made of reeds." Reed models plus wall hangings were sold as souvenirs and David had bargained for, and bought, a lovely tapestry.

That evening, we found a friendly restaurant in the dug-up main street. We were beginning to recover our appetites and we ordered a plate of fish and chips between us, the fish having been freshly caught in Lake Titicaca. As we ate, we were entertained by an excellent group of four young men playing a variety of instruments.

On the way back to the hotel, I said to David "I'm sure I can hear music playing." "Let's go and investigate," he suggested. We followed the sound and found a street hung with bunting and youngsters dancing round a huge bonfire in the middle of the road. "Is this a special celebration?" we asked an onlooker, thinking it was a local fete. "Yes," he told us, "it's the end of winter. Stay and join us."

Most of the dancers were in their teens and twenties but they were really friendly and welcomed us into the group. We stayed for about an hour before returning to the hotel, very impressed with Puno and the warmth and hospitality of the local people.

Day 21. Friday 23rd September.

Early the next morning, we set off by coach in the direction of Bolivia. It would be a long journey that day and to pass the time, Carol asked whether there were any questions about Peru before we left the country. Michael and Lynne asked her whether she had ever come across the Sendero Luminoso, the Shining Path guerillas, who had been in the news intermittently for several years but about whom very little had been heard recently.

Carol told us that she herself had never seen the guerillas and that since their leader had been captured some months earlier, there had been no problems. However, her predecessor had been on a tour coach that had been stopped by the Sendero Luminoso. They had demanded money from all the passengers and when one or two seemed reluctant to hand theirs over, they had held a gun to the tour guide's head and threatened to kill her if the tourists did not co-operate. After they had collected their booty, they left the coach taking the tour guide with them at gunpoint and she imagined the worst until, about half a mile down the road, they released her and made their escape and she was able to rejoin the tour.

After about two hours driving, we came to the small town of Juli, 80km from Puno. Here, the coach parked for a short time on the main square, outside the Church of San Pedro which happened to be close to the public conveniences.

The church looked very old and had an impressive bell tower at one end. In front of the church was an area of flat land, separated from the pavement by a double row of steps. All along these steps sat a row of women, some with young children and each with a pile of woven blankets and wall hangings. They vied with one another to attract our attention and we purchased two wall hangings as gifts for friends back in England. There were a few stalls in the square and we replenished our vital stock of water before rejoining the coach and continuing on our way across the Altiplano.

A few miles further on, we saw a church about a hundred yards from the road, where the local community was out in force celebrating the first day of Spring. We paused by the roadside for a few minutes and saw that they had a large band accompanying the singing and dancing. The dancing was well synchronised and involved high kicks and a twirling of skirts as the dancers moved in interweaving rows. We wanted to watch more closely but Carol thought we would be seen as unwelcome intruders.

From a little further on, the road ran close to the shore of Lake Titicaca which reflected the sky and shone a clear blue against the barren, drab landscape. As we neared the border with Bolivia, Carol asked us all to put away our cameras and video equipment and warned us not to speak to or smile at the Customs officers on either side of the border crossing in case it was taken in the wrong way. At the border, we queued to have our passports stamped, first in Peru and then, having walked across the border, in Bolivia.

Sillustani chullpas

Selling wall hangings at Juli

Making a reed boat

Reed boats

10

LAKE TITICACA AND LA PAZ

From the border, a cobbled road ran to the town of Copacabana where we stopped for lunch. This was an excellent meal, the best we had eaten since leaving Brazil. Near the restaurant, the town looked very poor and rundown but after the meal, we had a little free time and Carol suggested that we should walk up the hill towards the main square. Here, we were amazed suddenly to see the magnificent Basilica with its grand entrance gateway in white decorated with tiles of gold and black.

"The Basilica is famous for its Black Virgin," Carol told us. "There was just a small church here at first and the statue of the Virgin Mary in the church was given a darker skin so that black slaves working in the nearby Potosi silver mines could identify more easily with the Christian religion. The Virgin's statue, which dates back to the 16th century, quickly gained a reputation for performing miracle cures and Copacabana became a place of pilgrimage. It was then decided that the statue deserved to be housed in a cathedral and construction of the Basilica began at the start of the 17th century. The altars are made of silver from the Potosi mines."

Outside, the Basilica was sparkling white with Moorish domes. Inside, the style was baroque and the surrounds of the main altar were very ornate and covered with gold leaf. The altar of the Black Virgin was upstairs and here the altar was of pure silver and easier to appreciate because the surroundings were less flamboyant. The Virgin sat in the centre of the altar encased in glass and it is believed that, were the statue ever to be moved from the Basilica, the result would be the disastrous flooding of Lake Titicaca.

"Every year on Good Friday," Carol told us, "pilgrims come to Copacabana from miles around and follow the Stations of the Cross up the hill known as Calvary. At the top of the hill, they burn incense and buy miniatures of the Black Virgin to bring them health, good fortune and protection in the coming year. At dusk, a replica of the Black Virgin is carried in a candlelit procession through the town from the cathedral. People bring models of cars, houses and other items they would like to possess for these to be blessed by the Virgin in the hope that she will grant them the real thing at some time in the future. Before the pilgrims return home, their cars and lorries are decorated with brightly coloured garlands of plastic flowers and are blessed with alcohol for a safe journey."

While we were going round the Basilica, all our luggage had been unloaded from the Peruvian bus and tied on to the roof of the much smaller Bolivian bus in which we now continued our journey. From Copacabana, the road deteriorated into a single lane dirt track with very occasional passing places. This was the main Peruvian-Bolivian Highway.

Carol told us that outside La Paz, the capital, there is only one paved road in the whole of Bolivia which runs a distance of 300 km from La Paz. Luckily, we met only one other vehicle which pulled off the track for us as we followed the road up into the hills.

From above, we were able to look back across the flat plains surrounding Lake Titicaca, the only high ground in front of us being the peaks of two hills, one of which was Calvary, jutting out into the lake at Copacabana.

Lake Titicaca, over 230 km long from north-west to south-east, is the second largest lake in the whole of South America. We were traversing the mountains by what should have been a short route to reach the narrowest part of the lake, where vehicles cross by raft between east and west saving several hours journey. Unfortunately, part of the track had crumbled away and we were sent on a diversion that added a couple of hours to our journey.

We had a couple of brief stops to take photographs and to stretch our legs. The air at this altitude was very clear and we could see for miles across the azure-blue waters of the lake.

At last we reached the ferry terminal where the toilets were the only ones we had to pay for while in South America and were also the dirtiest, with no paper and no water whatsoever. Our bus waited in the queue of traffic waiting to cross on the raft and it was soon clear that there would be a long delay.

In view of this, Carol arranged for us to take an excursion across the lake. Our group split into two and we climbed aboard two motor boats which set off on a wonderful trip to the Island of the Sun, the legendary birthplace of Manco Capac, the first Inca. The journey lasted for about an hour and a half, the sun surprisingly warm, the water calm and the sky and lake a deep blue, separated by the snow-capped mountains of the Cordillera Real in the distance. We eventually reached the island and walked up the jetty past two magnificent examples of reed boats. Each of these carried a hut on its back like an enormous snail; one had the head of a bird, the other the head of an animal.

"The Island of the Sun was originally named Titicaca meaning "Rock of the Puma", after a rock on the island sacred to the local Indians," our guide from the motor boat told us. "The pre-Incan people of the Altiplano believed that their own gods and the sun itself had risen from the lake which was therefore sacred. The first Inca took advantage of this legend by saying that he and his sister, who was also his wife, were Children of the Sun and had been created on the Island of the Sun, whereupon the local people readily believed him and accepted him as their ruler. Surprisingly enough, this story is still believed today."

We walked up the hill from the harbour to a little souvenir shop where we met one of the men who had sailed with Thor Heyerdahl on the Kon Tiki expedition and who had helped in the building of Ra II. A replica of the reed boat stood outside the shop, sail billowing in the wind, the reed figurehead roaring in silent defiance. Behind the shop, a boat builder was at work constructing a new boat, tightening the strings that lash the reeds together.

"It takes three weeks to make a boat," explained our guide. "Unfortunately, the tradition is dying out because very few young people are interested in learning these skills." The boat builder we were watching was aged 75 and another boat builder was aged 101. Before we left, Shelagh bought a little reed boat and a reed llama as presents for her nieces.

As we left the island, the sun was setting and the temperature dropped rapidly. The wind rose and the water turned choppy. Our guide spread a tarpaulin over the boat which provided some shelter from the wind but despite huddling together for warmth, we were all chilled to the marrow by the time we arrived at the eastern shore, near a hotel, and staggered stiffly off the boat and on to the bus.

By this time it was 7pm. Before we set off on our journey again, the hotel very kindly provided each of us with a freshly-baked hot roll which warmed our hands and filled our stomachs.

From the lake, there was still a two hour journey before us and we were thankful that we had our alpaca sweaters, hats and gloves in the coach. Even so, it was almost impossible to get warm. Then at about 9pm, we came over the mountains and suddenly there below us stretched La Paz, a vision of sparkling lights that immediately made us forget the cold and our tiredness as we gazed at the beautiful sight. We slowly made our way down into the bowl of lights to the city centre.

We went straight to our hotel located on the Prado, the main street of the city, and unloaded the luggage from the roof of the bus. Then, leaving the luggage with Reception, we set off at about 9.30pm for our final meal together as a group. Carol had done her best and booked us a table at a restaurant specialising in traditional meals but by that time, many of us were too tired to want to eat much.

David and I skipped the starter course which was tiny fried sardines and rice soup. The main course was a choice of llama meat or guinea pig. We both decided to try llama as the thought of guinea pig put us off. This was a mistake!

There was a long wait for the food to arrive and when it finally came, the llama meat looked like burnt fried onion and was served with black potatoes. "Because the meat is so tough," Carol told us, "it is first boiled for several hours before being baked in the oven for a few more hours. Finally, it is cut into thin strips and fried to make it edible." We would query the 'edible' bit.

Those who had ordered guinea pig had it served flattened out with its legs spread out on either side and looking completely dried out. Again it was served with black potatoes. Several people complained that their meal was cold so Carol said "Pass all your plates up and I'll ask for the food to be reheated." When it was eventually returned, about half an hour later, it was lukewarm, ideal for food poisoning.

"My dinner is still cold," complained Jean. The waiter marched over to her, put his hand down flat on the food to test the temperature and said, "No, it isn't!" Jean refused to touch her meal after that and who could blame her. David also refused to try his but I tasted mine and found it very tough and chewy with the flavour of burnt salty bacon. This put me off eating any more. The final course was a strange-tasting fizzy fruit salad.

We had paid an extortionate price for this disastrous meal which was nothing but a tourist rip-off! It had cost each of us eight times as much as the excellent meal we had had the previous night, which had included entertainment. By this time, however, we were past caring and only too pleased when we finally arrived back at our hotel at 2am, absolutely exhausted.

Day 22. Saturday 24th September.

The next morning, we had packed our cases ready to leave for the airport at 2pm. Seven of us were returning to England, because unfortunately our jobs did not allow for more than three weeks holiday at the same time. The rest of the group were continuing their travels with a further two weeks exploring Bolivia and Paraguay, spending two days at the Iguassu Falls where they would also visit the Argentinian side of the Falls, before returning to Rio de Janeiro from where they would fly home.

We were all having breakfast together before taking a morning tour of La Paz which started at 8.30am when Carol came over with some bad news. "I've just been told that the President of Bolivia will be flying from the airport this afternoon," she said. "This means that your flight back to England has been brought forward and you will now have to leave for the airport at 11am. Unfortunately, there won't be enough time for you to take the city tour." We all exchanged addresses and Shelagh gave us both a hug, saying "You must come and stay with me in Winnipeg next summer. I'll write to you and send you photos from the rest of the trip." We waved goodbye to our friends, promising to keep in touch as they set off on their coach trip round La Paz.

Jack, Jean, Michael and Lynne all decided to relax and take it easy in the hotel for the next few hours. James wanted to buy some last minute presents so David and I set off by ourselves to see as much as we could in a short time. "Have you a map, please?" we asked the ladies at Reception "and is there anything nearby that we should see?" "I'm sorry" we were told , "we haven't any maps but if you turn left out of the hotel and follow the Prado, you'll come to the city centre."

The Prado was a stately main road with wide mosaic pavements in the area near our hotel and three traffic lanes in either direction, separated by a wide central reservation. The city looked very clean and modern with tall blocks of offices in concrete and glass between the hotels. Up the side streets, however, there were cracked, uneven paving stones and the buildings became older and more dilapidated the higher we climbed away from the main road. Between the buildings, we could see the mountains rising on all sides, their lower slopes covered by the poorer suburbs, to which the sparkling morning sunshine lent an air of beauty.

Despite being at a height of 13,000 feet, there were palm trees growing in the street and in a park by the Prado and we were told by the local people that this was made possible by the city's proximity to the Equator and the shelter provided by the surrounding mountains. The sky was a light blue overhead and the air held a wonderful clarity of light.

We followed the main road gently uphill until we came to the Cathedral. On the plaza outside the Cathedral, a band was holding a last minute rehearsal in preparation for a procession through the city. There were about twenty drummers, ten cymbal players and numerous pipers and marchers, all smartly dressed in navy and grey, the girl marchers wearing very short navy skirts and white boots. We were told that the procession was being organised by the local Lions Club in aid of charity.

Behind the Cathedral was a craft market where we saw some lovely carvings. Unfortunately, we only had a handful of loose change left and we decided to use this to buy some Bolivian stamps in the Post Office. On our way back to the hotel, we met James, who had already bought seven pairs of earrings as presents to take home, choosing yet another pair, either for his sister or his girlfriend. He asked for our opinion so we helped him make his selection and he returned with us to the hotel.

An eight-seater minibus arrived for us promptly at 11am and we left for the airport. The traffic in La Paz was horrendous. When the lights turned green, the traffic edged across until it was completely blocking the road so that when the lights changed again, the traffic in the opposite direction had nowhere to go. Everyone then tried to get into the outside lanes to squeeze through whenever there was a small gap between cars. Our driver informed us that the traffic was usually this bad by mid-morning and we could appreciate why there would have been no time for a city tour.

Eventually we left the traffic congestion in the city centre and began to climb towards the airport, where we were treated to views across the city to the snow-capped mountains beyond. At the airport, we went to the check-in desk where the girl eyed David's bow and arrows that had been too long to pack into his case. "You can't take those as hand luggage," she said. "I'll get a label put round them and they can go into the hold with the other luggage. They'll be quite safe there."

It did not seem long before we were boarding the aircraft and taking off. The views were wonderful as the 'plane circled the mountains, gradually gaining altitude in the thin air.

On the way to Sao Paulo in Brazil, we landed for what should have been a brief stop. However, the Guard of Honour was lined up about ten feet from our aircraft and we sat and watched the President of Bolivia arrive with two companions on a small private airplane. He was greeted and hurried to the airport buildings before we were allowed to take off. From here, we had an uneventful flight to Sao Paulo and, eventually, to London.

We had had a marvellous trip, rich with a variety of landscapes, climates, cultures and cuisines. We had had some memorable experiences and had made many new friends with whom we hoped to keep in touch. It was now time to return to everyday life and to dream of our next exciting exploration holiday.